Green Carrot - America's Work Visa Crisis

RAJIV DABHADKAR

Copyright © 2014 Rajiv Dabhadkar

All rights reserved.

ISBN: 1500929107
ISBN-13: 978-1500929107

DEDICATION

my parents for teaching me to walk ..

my wife and my daughter for teaching me to run ..

CONTENTS

	Acknowledgments	I
	Foreword	Pg # 4
Chapter 1 :	Bodyshopping – Cash for Visa	Pg # 8
Chapter 2 :	Twelve Years A Slave	Pg # 34
Chapter 3 :	Banged Up On Christmas	Pg # 45
Chapter 4 :	Being A Foreigner Home	Pg # 52
Chapter 5 :	Carrot Of A Green Card	Pg # 66
Chapter 6 :	Pursuit Of HappYness	Pg # 84
Chapter 7 :	Lobbying For Change	Pg # 105
Chapter 8 :	Justice Delayed, Justice Denied	Pg # 122
Chapter 9 :	Stepping Up The Mandate	Pg # 133
Chapter 10 :	Back To The Future	Pg # 159
Chapter 11 :	Happy Feet Partnership	Pg # 174
Chapter 12 :	A Final Word	Pg # 188

ACKNOWLEDGMENTS

Writing a book is similar to entering a long term relationship with an obsessive partner. Throughout the time it took to write this book, life went on: hospitalization and the isolation, court cases in different continents, divorce and the separation, births, deaths and even witnessing live the attacks of 9/11.

Throughout it all, the book and the purpose remained constant. Some stayed on, others left, every roadblock only strengthening the determination further. Therefore, I'd like to thank the people that made it possible to focus on the book to the exclusion of nearly everything else and publicly acknowledge their contributions.

My parents, who have supported and encouraged me throughout, even when I was little more than a reclusive houseguest hunched over the computer while recovering from my illness. At every roadblock, they have been there, either as patient listeners or as witness to the occasional emotional outbursts. Without their support I would not have been able to drill down on life's facing challenges and weed out chunks of negativities from my life.

I cannot forget to mention, my appreciation for my wife, without whose memories I would not have continued on the mission mandate of my organization for twelve long years. By not allowing me a closure to the hurt, she has inadvertently dared me to continue, just enough to keep me tuned to the goal within!

My special thanks to Malia Politzer for her editing of the crucial initial chapters, those sensitive yet important years in the beginning of my life story.

To my dear friend, co-founder of my organization and mentor, S.B Swaminathan, who has always been on the frontline consistently nagging, buttering and dragging my ego to make this dream possible.

I am also lucky to have a whole community behind me in the creation of this book. Everyone who has ever been on the F-1, L-1, or the H-IB visa in many ways shares part of the credit. You know who you are. You helped support me in the difficult efforts to try and clarify my thoughts while we worked together over the years and also while writing and rewriting this book. We may not have met but interacted on discussion boards, emails and telephone conversations over the years.

Special thanks to Hari Amaravadi, Gaurav Yadav, Ashish Srivastava - friends and team members of NOSTOPS who have been kind enough to read and re read the chapters. Away from one another in different time zones, your feedback was timely and prompt. Your many questions, comments and reactions have been extremely valuable in the shaping of this book.

To Gaurav, for not only having spent a considerable amount of time and self less efforts in designing of the book cover but also for staying in constant touch with his words of encouragement.

To Donna Conroy and Mike Rothschild of Bright Future Jobs; Roy Lawson, Kim Berry and John Miano of The Programmer's Guild Of America; and countless others who have been supportive of the NOSTOPS journey. Without you, these twelve years would simply not have been possible!

I also want to acknowledge all those people who see me through this book; and to all those who provided support, talked things over, read, wrote, offered comments, allowed me to quote their remarks.

Last and not least: I beg forgiveness of all those who have been with me over the course of the years and whose names I have failed to mention.

FOREWORD

When we speak of people migration in the context of social reality – there exists a cultural disconnect that creates social inequality amongst workers.

After spending most of my adult life working as a migrant worker and studying the process of human migration, I have written this book with a focus on issues most commonly faced by Indian workers while working overseas. The book is dedicated to the real life issues in the process of human migration. It discusses people movement that is tied to immigration and trade policy, where workers are treated as a commodity and is not just about selling a product or a service. It is about finding the future. It explores the future of the workers, the corporations and the society at large.

The primary objective however lies in finding the future. Not just any future in general, but specific futures for the individuals under the care of policies that govern people movement. The focus is the future, in the sense that it makes a prediction about where the future lies and then takes specific steps to make that future happen.

That's where the subject of human migration comes in.

The globalized political and economic system creates illegality by displacing people and then denying the workers' their rights and equality as they have to do what they have to do in order to survive. Globalization forces people into migration into countries where the ideas of divide and rule have been codified as a "legal" justification for the injustices. Inequality therefore is re-created and re introduced by a global economic system.

In the realm of social reality – this social inequality creates a caste system, where one class of workers is pitted against the other for personal gain. Where when one side of the coin gets tainted, the other side shines brightly, putting the society at large in a conundrum.

This book examines the function of 'social inequality' in a modern world of high-tech guest workers and India's increasing dependence on exporting people to the labor pool in the global North. This book is titled "Green Carrot – America's Work Visa Crisis" in recognition of this reality.

While Indian workers serving with employers in the United States has been used as a case study, it aims to drive home a point - Should the human migration exports rest only on the economic needs or should they be more focused on the human rights of its workers?

Through the book an attempt is made to explore the politics of the debate over immigration and trade policies between India and the United States. It analyses the guest worker programs and recounts my own experiences as a guest worker and also the personal experiences of others involved.

The book examines closely the cultural factors associated with the brokerage of intellectual capital and rights to intellectual property - two distinct yet, vulnerable areas in the political debate on immigration reform. The book examines body shopping as a business model that promotes the brokerage of intellectual capital and ends with the need for innovation, bringing focus on generating intellectual property – identified as the root for immigration reform.

The book begins with looking at what it means to be caught in the caste system in India – where economic status is often considered as an easy alternative to migration. It further examines what it means to be an indentured guest worker in labor bondage with a foreign employer - how immigration status is used to keep people vulnerable, to criminalize them and punish them when they try to improve their conditions.

The narrative travels to examine how the visa status is used to control the movement of its foreign employee and how the 'brokerage of intellectual capital' allows subjugation for personal gain and its consequences on family life.

The book traces back in history to explore America's dependence on foreign labor and examines how the present day system of body shopping in fact creates an economic system that benefit from the changes caused by labor displacement, and also benefits from the labor displacement it produces, especially those on the foreign work visas.

It traces the development of the employer lobby set up to win the expansion of the work visa programs. How the immigration policies have all but been about low salaries for foreign workers, excluding the local workers from competing for jobs thus dividing the workforces.

The book narrates my journey from the streets of Navi Mumbai where I lived as a homeless after my decade long stay in the United States. It narrates the beginning of my journey in the space of seeking rights for workers – those that were indentured and serving involuntarily; those beholden to their employers. The narrative progresses to convey my participation in generating awareness that lead to a few changes to the policy over the past decade. It details the journey from a whistleblower to documenting existence of fraud and abuse within the foreign worker community. It succinctly tries to detail the arrival of a visa reform bill to prevent fraud and abuse of foreign workers on guest worker visa programs. The narrative has also tried to bring attention to the democratic nature of judiciary in both United States as well as India.

Towards the end, an attempt is made to understand the globalization needs of nations that require changes to the trade policies, which are treated in isolation. Human migration is a derivative of these trade policies but the laws are debated and designed individually. Technology increases human interaction and the resulting collapsing of borders increases human migration. It looks at the way forward by examining factors that align to these needs of a globalized society.

Finally the book suggests some alternatives, always the hardest part in the immigration debate. It concentrates on some of the most progressive ideas, which have been put forward by immigration and human rights activists. It advocates a need for an open transparent system - an open verified worker registry for India to align itself to the needs of employers globally.

GREEN CARROT

1 BODY SHOPPING – CASH FOR VISA

It was the morning of September 11th. I took the morning 8:05 from Harrison. Traveling through the underground tunnel, beneath the Hudson River, it was an easy commute with just 3 stops in between. It was rush hour and I made a bee line to get onto the escalator on the mezzanine floor. As I stepped on the escalator, I could feel the cool air blowing into the tunnel from above.

Working as an Information Architect for Merrill Lynch, the days were routine and the commute easy. A 20 minute underground train ride beneath the Hudson River to the Word Trade Center, and I was right beneath my office building. An escalator ride followed by an elevator and I was literally at my desk. It was a convenient 30 minute - home to desk travel. A coffee and a smoke at a local new stand across the building was a routine, giving me enough time to shake off the lethargy. Lunch usually was sitting by the waterfront overlooking the Hudson, in the warmth of the winter sunlight. The city life was easy and I was beginning to enjoy it.

My office was on the 11th floor in the North tower. Coming out of the escalator, I looked at my wrist watch, and it said 8:47 am. I still had time to get into office. An elevator ride up, and I will be lost from the world outside, at least for another couple of hours. Leslie, my manager, was a task master. She'd soon being going on a maternity leave and she expected a lot to be completed by then. And I wasn't complaining. As an indentured worker bound by an employer sponsored visa can never complain…or at least shouldn't! I was happy to do it. As a foreign worker in the United States, a place I had come with my wife to escape the pressure of a conservative culture to build a new future, long working hours were just a building block to the American Dream.

I know I should have rushed up – I was running late. But I decided to linger a few minutes, and indulge in a quick cigarette break before logging in for the daily grind. Here the entire building was a non smoking zone. A cigarette break, required traveling from the 11th floor, walk about 100 meters and passing through security. It was cumbersome. A big change from what I was so used to while at Bedminster. The quiet, serene and quaint atmosphere of the country side was now replaced by the city noise; office goers, employees of mom n pop restaurants pushing flyers into your hands, hustlers, peddlers, beggars, tourists, yellow cabs, and the maddening noise of honking cars stuck in traffic. Thankfully, I never felt the need to get on the city streets, if I didn't want to. That's what I really liked about working here.

Branded cigarettes were expensive and the costs were different in different states. Just outside the building, the newsstand owned by an Indian offered the same cigarettes at half the price. As I made my way through the crowd to get outside the building, I could see Mansukhbhai, already busy with his morning customers. Dodging in between the rush hour traffic, I crisscross over to the other side, land my $5 bill on the counter and wait expectantly for the usual coffee with cream n sugar and a pack of Marlboro lights.

What happened next would shake the world, and set into action a chain of events that would destroy everything I had been working towards—unraveling my dreams thread by thread. I heard the sound of a large engine followed by a loud shattering noise, people screams, and screeching of brakes. I was pushed and even before I could realize, I was lying flat on the pavement. A crowd of people were running away from me. "Fuck" I said, lying there dazed. I glanced to my right. I had missed hitting my head on the fire hydrant by inches.

I am still lying horizontal on the pavement as I look up. Next to me is a crowd of people looking up towards the sky. The sky is dark red, surrounded by billowing black smoke clouds. And then, I see the bottom half and the tail of a silver airplane jutting out from the building.

"Oh God …. NO", the man standing next to me shouted. He was wearing a red flannel shirt and dark blue jeans. From my vantage, I saw a small shape, like a bird—but as it grew closer it took on the proportions of a human form. People were jumping from the building. I was just less than 20 meters away from the revolving doors of Tower I—out of which I had exited just minutes ago. The falling form grew closer—I could make out the shape of a woman wearing a grey suit, falling from the sky. She was screaming. Her body made a muffled thump as she hit the pavement, creating a small crater in the pavement. As I stared, shocked, she was soon joined by others bodies, jumping from the towers.

I am completely senseless and numb. It was as though the muffled thuds of bodies falling were the sounds of my own heartbeat. I just lay there numbed with the horror. People had begun running away from the building as I was trying to get up

The screams got louder, louder screams, people running, people run over, utter chaos …. I realized that another plane had crashed in the World Trade Center. I thought this could be one freak accident in the history of the United States, when suddenly someone grabbed me by my arm and yanked me. "Run!" He yelled

And I too ran … ran for my life…. ran for safety… I forgot my laptop bag; I just got up and ran!! My black suit wide open, buttons ripped, torn at the left elbow, white shirt soled with sweat, wet black trousers …I sprinted like a timid animal chased by a predator ; I ran in fear…I ran to save myself…. From what, I still had no idea, but I ran because every other person around me was also running. I ran because the man in the red flannel shirt had commanded me to do so.

I was nearly 3 blocks when I heard a very loud rumbling noise. I almost ran over someone ahead of me, who had stopped to turn to see behind us. I turned around and looked. What I saw, gave me the shivers, and created a deeply etched memory that would continue to haunt me for the years to come. The entire building was beginning to crumble. A cloud of white debris and dust concealed the square of pavement where I'd been lying but a moment before. And then, the building folded in on itself, roaring and rumbling with larger chunks of debris flying. In a matter of seconds, the World Trade Center twin towers were no more. One of hundreds, I began to run again.

It was close to 11:00 am when I reached mid town Manhattan. I had walked nearly 28 blocks. I heard from many on my way, that this indeed was a terrorist attack and I was deeply worried. I thought of the safety of my wife and child. Numbed, I took out my cell phone, and compulsively dialed my wife's phone number as I walked—all circuits busy, New York was in complete chaos. The entire city reverberated with the sirens of Police vehicles, Fire Trucks and Ambulance Vans.

I reached home a little after 4 pm. She was standing by the window, phone in hand. As soon as she saw me coming, she went inside. Moments later, I see her come running towards me bare foot. She stopped mid way, just a few meters away. With the baby tucked under the arm, perched on her right hip, there she stood… her left palm over her mouth, fighting her tears. Moments later, as we embraced, I could see her face was puffy and her eyes red-rimmed.

We sat down on the beige couch in the living room. She told me about things, that she heard on the television, of things that I had not known, of her desperation trying to reach me, of the calls received from our families back home. I shared my eye witness account of what happened and how I ran, lost my laptop in the panic. I spoke about the chaos, the people screaming, jumping off the buildings, and how I had walked home, a distance of about 30 miles.

That night of September 11th, 2001, we slept in the living room, spreading our mattresses out in front of the television set. We stayed awake, watching the news, as slowly the facts of the event were unfolded. It was indeed a terror attack on America. It was nearly midnight, as we lay on our mattresses, wondering if those we knew working in the city were safe. What we saw on the television, was so very like a scene from a movie, we hoped it would get over soon. We were immersed in our own thoughts as we watched silently.

Just as I was drifting to sleep, Sujata moves closer to give me a good night kiss and whispers- "You must be really tired, you walked so much today. Take a day off from work tomorrow and rest"

My eyes snap open to meet hers. I do not know, how long we had held the gaze looking into one another's wide eyes, as a second dreadful fact sunk in – "I no longer had a job to go to."

I had met Sujata way back in 1989, in Mumbai. In a class of 38 students, she was an integral part of our project group. She led the group not only due to her fancy looks rather because of her articulate and punctual nature. As our course progressed, and we spend time on our project work, we often found ourselves working together alone. She was ambitious with a warm smile and down to earth as well, a rare combination. She conducted herself with an air of confidence that a few considered to be snobbish. My innocent tease would endlessly be cut short, but the fondness for her stayed nevertheless. Before we knew it, we often had dinners together in restaurants, and caught up on weekends for movies. Or simply took a walk by the seashore to watch the sun set, sharing, exchanging our views, values, ideals and goals in life. She had become a great friend with common dreams and expectations from life. She was also charmingly beautiful, compassionate and a sensitive girl.

At the age of 21, while a majority of my friends that I grew up with were preparing for their higher studies in America, I was still finding myself. I continued to be the sales man that I was, selling fire extinguishers door to door to those that didn't need one. I wouldn't have taken it up, had it not been for Sujata's insistence, forcing me to earn enough to pay for my own course fees.

As we neared the end of our semester, we had understood one another well. We understood, we had a lot in common. Apart from the class projects that we did together, we acknowledged that we shared a common identity, in terms of our expectations from life, from our career, from family. Like me, she too was the youngest of her siblings. She too was a second generation migrant in the city of Mumbai. Both our parents had moved in the city for work, detached from their respective sources of origin. She had received an offer from Hindustan Lever, in Chennai as a management intern and would be leaving soon. She too would be moving in a new city, facing newer challenges unique to a new place and eventually blend in her new work environment and gradually detach self from the city she grew in.

It was a little after 8 on a Thursday evening, as we sat on the white marbled foot steps outside our college's main entrance. Resting our backs on the closed entrance doors, we sat in the silence of the evening's darkness. It was a romantic evening. The rush hour of South Mumbai had ebbed and the streets were less noisy. It was a difficult moment for us, as we sat in silence. We were meeting for the last time to bid a final goodbye. She was just a friend, but a dear friend that I may never see again. We could stay in touch, and possibly meet in the future. Even then, there was a weird heart ache. An occasional streak of street light falling on her face, peeking through the tree leaves dancing in the evening sea breeze, and I could clearly see the swelling tear drops in her eyes. The lump in the throat made it difficult for either of us to speak.

"So now you can concentrate on going to America too, just like your friends. Now that I won't be there to harass you" – She said almost in a whisper, breaking the silence. As she struggled to hide her tears, she continued – "Study for the entrance exams. I will send you money for the fees."

"America? I was thinking of looking for a job in Chennai" – I replied. The tears were now distinctly visible. The long pause and the discomfort of facing up to reality had finally sunk in. We were sitting close, with our shoulders touching one another. As she wiped the falling tear with the back of her palm, she said clearing her throat - "No America is better. There will be no family to interfere. We will never be accepted here. Kids in such situations, grow up with social distrust".

A lot transpired in those brief moments. As our hearts leaped acknowledging acceptance, life's new path was being laid out right in front of us. We were to design the architecture of our life's own destiny.

Ever since the memorable evening, Sujata and I were inseparable, synchronizing every minute detail, consulting and occasionally falling back on the other for advice. We were not only creating our identities together, but also defending it, as a couple; especially when our families disapproved our growing closeness. Disapproved because of the conflicting ideals of our family's belief systems that sat at the core deciding the fate of our bond. Conflicts those were specific to culture, that migrants face, when uprooted and detached from their culture's source of origin.

I believe, migrants everywhere, bring with them their own beliefs and build lifestyles that form a community, all in search of a cultural identity. To the migrants, the desire of belonging to a community is as important and necessary to their survival as is the need to find work, or to escape challenges. The understanding of mutual assistance makes it easier for the members of a community to come together and organize themselves. Members of a community also like to save their language so that it lives on and continues into the future. This participatory democracy finds its roots in the indigenous village life, which is also a part of the migrant's culture. Also, migrants by virtue of their new established identity are far more industrious than their children as they not only pursue in the creation and the preservation of their culture, but also by making frequent remittances to their source of origin.

How else could people maintain and recreate their identity when they become physically distant from the towns that are its source? As new generations grow up detached from their culture's point of origin, will they be willing to accept and reproduce the traditions of their parents? Community therefore lies at the heart of the questions posed by migration.

But to our families, migration had its costs. Detached from their own sources of origin, they themselves struggled to keep up with the traditional cultural practices and the language. As migrant parents, they too did their best to offer us children a mix of these traditions and customs as well as the language that kept our identities alive, in a city far from our respective cultural sources. They constantly worried if we could not only embrace the traditions, but also be able to transfer the same to our children. Our respective families were staunch believers of the traditions and the customs that they belonged to. They had succeeded in keeping their social identity, in a new city and expected us to continue with the cultural priorities as well. As is the case, with the older generations, these beliefs system held them together in a community and marrying someone outside of the caste, or outside of the community was a threat as that would mean to break away from the tradition held by our families for generations to come.

In our case, the breaking away from our respective cultures was obvious especially because they were distinctly different. Our families had different beliefs, belonged to different cultures with lifestyles completely apart from one another.

But despite these cultural and domestic challenges both of us brought with us a high degree of flexibility and a strong ability to adapt. We had a strong ability to identify ourselves with our professional dreams. To begin life anew, to be accepted, by our families, to be bound emotionally, the need to be professionally secure was a shared common identity that we carefully nurtured.

And when the going got tough, she stayed committed through out it all standing by me like a rock when our families were against us getting married - accusing us of polluting our respective cultures.

When the priority of wanting to see their children settled in a comfortable employment, only to eventually get us married was the highest, falling in love with someone out of the community was not taken in lighter vein. Even though we tried to keep in touch, despite the resistance from our families, it was getting imperative that we sought a common ground to convince our families. Her mobility was greatly restricted and soon marriage proposals within her community were arranged to curb our growing closeness. Her job prospects dwindled and moving out of the city to a new position at Chennai was swiftly declined.

Attempts made to my family too were refuted. It was now critical to create possibilities that would allow us one last chance. And to seek at finding a common goal both the families could identify with. And this one last chance had to be one that could give us a life together forever, away from our respective sources of resistance.

A new beginning in America promised that life; a life that offered a common goal of financial freedom, where both the families would also be the eventual beneficiaries, was accepted with grace. Even though at logger heads for a little more than two years, we were eventually able to win consent from both the families.

Okay..to be honest, we won consent from 'almost all' important decision makers from our respective sides. A decision was made, and we were to be given exactly two years to prove our intent. I was to depart to The Americas, and 'settle down' before a marriage date could be finalized.

Despite the agreement, subtle taunts continued. Barely two months out of the country, and her marriage proposals begun with complete ignorance to the spoken word. It therefore became imperative to completely disconnect with our respective families, and embark on a life together without the nagging interference of our families.

Back then, it was fairly easy to get to the United State of America as a student. I presume, it still is, if the intent is genuine. Back then, I didn't really want to leave, but then I had to go in order to come back and deliver on my promise.

Arriving in the United States of America as an International student on the F-1 visa, I was enrolled in the Master's in Computer Science program in January 1991. With a tuition waiver and a 20 hour per week on campus employment, I was onto a great start in living the American dream. My college was just 3 miles from the Jersey shore at Monmouth. And the apartment was literally on the shore. A wooden boardwalk and the sand separated our apartment building from the sea. Famously known as the 'seven president's beach', the beach on the ocean was also a tourist destination. Motels and gift shops were the only commercial premises within walking distance.

It may sound a bit embarrassing today, but back then it was the pride to have lived like a pauper the first few months on arrival. I wanted to save enough to travel back and get married and bring back my wife to a new life. I did not own a car neither did I party on the weekends like many of my Indian friends. I not only shared a two bedroom apartment with eight other Indian students from the same college, I also worked at a motel from five in the morning until noon as a janitor changing bed sheets and cleaning the toilets. A job on campus in the afternoons and classes in the evening, I never did feel homesick the first few months. And the lowest of my grades were an

A minus !

Shortly, within the next six months, I delivered on a promise made - I finally got married to Sujata, my school sweetheart, in June the very same year. After courting her for three years, hiding from our families, convincing them to support the union, proving to them the good intent of living our lives together as a family and then finally marrying, our lives were full of joy. We were on top of the world. We believed that family resentments would not matter as much, as long as we lived up to their expectations of being financially secure. We were the first from either of our families to venture out of country, we were glad to embark on a new journey and a new destination allowing us together to live a life with dignity, respect and honor. To live in a country that tolerates who you were, irrespective of caste, creed, and country of origin, religious beliefs or skin color. The United States of America therefore seemed like an alternative to escape from the pressures of families, and build a life together.

Like many of our Indian friends with inter caste marriages, we too had adopted a few coping strategies against the psychological abuses flung by our respective families.

We detached and distanced ourselves from our families and lived independently, becoming satisfied with limited or no communication with the families or lived with a belief that there is no family to depend upon. We aimed to maintain a positive image about ourselves and were thankful of being together; thinking of the worst possible experiences in India, and selectively made social comparisons. While we maintained low expectations from families to curb the dissatisfaction and the disappointment, we accepted our non acceptance, and lived with the hope for the future by focusing on long-term goals, such as becoming professionally secure, or obtaining the green card. All the while, remaining cynical about the nature of our families and believing that their belief system itself is flawed. We tried to insulate ourselves from family and friends back home by forming a group of people around us facing similar circumstances, creating a social bulwark and a social buffer to air grievances amongst ourselves.

Over the last couple of years, away from our families, we had indeed built a new life for ourselves in a foreign land, that we called our new home. We showed up for all the festivals and events that the Indian community celebrated. We spent a great deal of time together. We enjoyed each and every moment of being in love. We took long drives, we exercised, we laughed, we fought, and we cried, we patched up, we confronted and we celebrated. In our best moments, we visited the temples or just stayed at home enjoying one another's company. The United States of America was our home because it promised us a life of respect and dignity. America was indeed, a home away from home.

It had been four years since our arrival and a little more than a year working on the H1-B visa. Working as a tech support analyst, for an American company in Long Island, New York., I was the only Indian, on a non-immigrant work visa. A daily train commute, two hours each way included a seven mile walk from the train station, irrespective of rain, sleet or snow. Working on my first job, as a tech support analyst, my pack check was miniscule, leaving me with $500, after taxes from my bi-monthly pay check. But, I was glad I had a job to go to, it was way better than having nothing at all. I had incurred a lot of debt as a student. Both of us had taken turns skipping a semester, and working full time in order to help pay the tuition fees, for the one taking full time courses. It was now my turn to pay for her remaining course fees and I was glad to do just that. Life was fulfilling back then, because despite the days struggle, we looked forward to being home together.

While we struggled, to establish ourselves in a foreign country, families back home, waited impatiently, to find us get settled; and to have a child. To the elite masses, to which our families belonged to, a visa to America was considered as a ticket to heaven. America, after all was a land of opportunity. Where else does money ooze out of the Automated Teller Machine, at the snap of a finger? At a time, when the Automated Teller Machines were available only at the vicinities of the top brass in India, the fantasy of deposit money in New York, and withdraw seven seas across, seemed too compelling. It cut through the dogma of "How are you guys doing? What time is it there now?"

Four years in the land of opportunity, without an increase to the size of our bank account or that to our family member count was a serious concern to our families, located exactly on the other side of the planet!

It has been a practice, for our families to interfere on personal matters from deciding the right time to conceive to how to raise a child. Young couples, such as us, distanced from our families, coupled with the day to day challenges of a foreign land, found this to be an invasion of our privacy. The hypocrisy continued because questioning or speaking against elders was considered disrespectful. We simply choose to ignore the sarcasm. Nevertheless, the pressure continued. We were pressurized into having a child and begin a family. We had the best critics, and we did all things possible to please them, just so we were accepted.

"Do you have a problem? Maybe you should get your sperms checked" my elder sister-in-law blasted on the telephone.

We both were twenty seven, when our daughter was born. Her birth was a testament to the commitment to love that we as parents shared. She was a result of this commitment, and so, we named her, our only child - 'Pranauti', which in Sanskrit means – 'a prayer born out of a commitment'.

As always, despite our families' wishes, we chose to have our daughter to be born in India. We wanted our child to be a naturalized citizen of the Republic Of Independent India. The reasons were many, but as parents - we wanted our daughter to be identified with her source, and to be able to know of her origin. Despite the challenges that we as parents went through, we believed, our daughter would be protected by our beliefs and grow up as an adult making her own decisions with regards to her citizenship status or the choice of her country of residence.

With my wife in India, and while I awaited the arrival of our newborn, I was searching in earnest for a job in or around New Jersey. Of all the available options in the North Eastern United States, the state of New Jersey was most preferred, only because it served two important aspects – first, an opportunity to be with the culture that we forcibly left behind. Second, the bountiful alternate employment opportunities, and other revenue sources, that act as temporary buffers when it was necessary to shield away from the visa sponsor abuse related ad-hoc unemployment. As per the American work visa laws, an employer that sponsors a foreign worker a work visa, must continue to pay the salary even during unemployment however most companies do not pay such a salary. It therefore becomes necessary to find alternate means of cash work – working under the table. Working in Indian restaurants or Indian owned motels, offer such opportunities in times of desperation.

Indians, by virtue of their kinship to fellow Indians, are among the fastest duplicators. Be it a new trend or a profitable business model. Within the close knit community, success is as much about money and reputation, as it is about religion and culture. The more successful you are, the more you do for the community you are a part of - the more reputation you gain. The quicker a successful business venture is duplicated the quicker is the return on investment. Be it the success of a dot com business by the famed hotmail's Sabeer Bhatia, the success in motel or convenience store businesses, or, as recent as the business of body shopping - importing workers from overseas, floating a software training institute, coaching them in-house and farming out these workers to work for American firms. Until the incident of 9/11 in the year 2001, petitions for work visas that required an American employer were seldom denied nor scrutinized anyways.

Having studied in America, I was finding it easy to get a job but difficult to find an employer that was willing to sponsor me a work visa. Back in 1992-93, American firms either did not know such a work visa was available or even if they did, they did not have the legal expertise in house to do the necessary paperwork and were too skeptical of using it. As a result, I was unable to find a direct employer that could sponsor me a work visa, and so a 'body shop' was the only available option.

A body shop is basically a company that offers a letter of employment, files a work visa petition of a foreign worker and out places them into a local American firm. The body shop then earns a commission for every hour worked by the foreign worker they have thus sponsored. Body shop's basically function as 'brokers of intellectual capital'. Body shopping was becoming popular because getting a work visa via such firms was fairly easy. As the practice of body shopping became popular, these body shops did not even require meeting or speaking with the hired worker overseas. These brokers, often operating as individuals charged a heavy recruiting fee in exchange for a work visa thus indirectly promoting unmonitored migration of human beings across borders. This unmonitored 'brokerage of intellectual capital" has today created a massive economic dent, simply because these firms and their agents could insource human talent from outside the United States and outsource them to local companies domestically without scrutiny.

The body shops had equal rights as the American firms that employed the foreign workers and so, the body shops controlled the movement and the activities of these workers. Because the immigration process was technical and complex, there was wide spread abuse without much scrutiny to look into the nature of illegal activities prevalent then. There weren't any investigations on abuse being reported either. This encouraged many unscrupulous fly-by-night individuals in creating fake companies to import unqualified candidates who mercilessly manipulated their documentation required towards procuring a work visa, in exchange for large sums of money. Visa scams and visa hustling were at its peak. A work visa could easily be procured in exchange for anything between 8 – 12 lakh rupees (16,000 – 24,000 $ US). The heavy sum in exchange for a work permit that guaranteed a 3 years no questions asked legal residence in The Americas was an excellent alternative to migration.

This made the process difficult for the genuine hard working candidates, who were less preferred by the recruiting agents overseas, against those willing to pay only to gain entry via fraudulent means and falsifying documents. Take for example the case of Prasanth Nair, a resident of Mumbai, and an engineering grad with over four years of work experience. He too wanted to live the American dream. Many of his college friends had reached The Americas and he too was hopeful that one day he too would reach the American shores. And live a dignified life, and call his widow mother to join him. But first, he had to be financially responsible. He had lost his father. His old mother and unmarried sister was still dependant on him. He had been approached by many companies that were willing to sponsor his H1-B visa; some were even companies where his friends worked.

With the family commitment taken care of, when he eventually did select a company to sponsor his work visa, he willingly sent the money to the company towards the visa petition fees. He promptly wired 2 lakh rupees (approximately 2,200 $) in 2008, towards which neither did he receive any confirmation of receipt of payment neither the promised visa. His employer simply vanished. Today, Prasanth works as a technical manager with Citigroup, and fondly travels across the globe on office visits.

Or take the example of Akhil. Akhil received an employment offer from Vision Systems Group (VSG), a company in New Jersey in 2007. Being the only son of a business man in Mumbai, he sends in his fees. In his case, it was 4000$. His visa too never came in. His employer simply forgot to file the papers within the stipulated deadline of October 1st;the date beyond which the H1-B applications were not accepted. Continued persistence, and in 2008, his employer filed the papers but the immigration department sent in an RFE (Request for Evidence), and applications of many prospective individuals like him that had paid the visa fees to VSG were rejected. Reason? – the company itself was found fraudulent. The company had been under audit and after the investigation, VSG was eventually shut down. Like Prasanth, Akhil too lost his money. Meanwhile, he enrolled in Sweden under the Erasmus Mundus program, and upon completion of his Master's program chose to apply for a US work visa again. At the interview, he was advised that he had been debarred from seeking a US visa for 3 years for falsifying in his immigration paperwork earlier through the body shop that was now nonexistent! Today, Akhil has gained his residency permit allowing him to stay in Europe permanently, is married and happily settled.

As the quantum of worker abuses and the related human rights violations increased, America continued to be burdened with additional resources and losing precious time in controlling the migratory flow, instead of fixing the policies preventing abuse that lie at the root of the indentured nature of the visa program. With an annual quota of 65,000, large corporations petition for work visas in large numbers and exhaust these work visa quotas. Firms' dependant on these work visas have grown into large corporations today and have amassed huge profits simply by virtue of brokering the talent gap, driving down wages and creating an inflated market demand.

But the H1-B program, not only is a means to transport illegal migrants alone, it is also a convenient system that permits employers to divide and segregate its workforce, resulting in the exclusion of local workers by preferring certain class of workers such as those from overseas on short term visas and those with limited rights. Those less qualified non deserving workers are pre qualified by the body shops overseas before their work visa is petitioned, and having limited ability to understand laws or even seeking rights becomes a solid value proposition to their visa sponsor employers.

While working with body shops allegedly depresses the wages of foreign workers, they simply bypass hiring of local citizens. Companies engaged in the business of body shopping often 'banked visas' for foreign workers, i.e., keeping the excess of approved H1-B workers in their home countries and sending them to the United States only as the need arises. The 'need' again is ambiguous, as we shall see in the following chapters.

But the real reason for body shops using the program is for personal gain. It allows for a convenient way to store illegal wealth across borders. There are many complexities to the H1-B program, many of which have been devised to necessitate America's need for foreign labor. But keeping to the fairness of the programs good intent, lets us look at how one single H1-B sponsored visa, can be profitable.

At the onset, it may be important to know that the H1-B visa program is a federal program however the visa sponsoring petitions filed by the companies are governed by the prevailing wage in the intended area of available work locally. Simply put, an employer in Idaho or Nebraska with a low living index compared to the states such as California and New York City where the standard of living is higher, could still get the 'labor approval', simply put 'permission to import a foreign worker', by simply proving that the local salary would be paid irrespective of the workers location nationwide.

Please note, that the H1-B program began in 1991, and in just five years, in 1996, because of the corporate lobbying, there was a change made to the "H1-B portability" clause, that allowed the sponsored foreign worker on H1-B visa to work at different locations on client sites, without requiring them to be paid the local salaries. Workers petitions were approved in low states but they were actually working in states where the cost of living was high. Many body shopping firms registered in Idaho, Maine, and Nebraska were getting approvals. And out placing these workers to companies in expensive cities at a much higher prevailing wage per hour.

It may be important to note that foreign workers are paid a fixed salary and the companies that sponsor them, the body shops, pocket the difference including the overtime pay. Keeping the costs low and selling talent at the highest possible premium was the key. Guest houses of such firms, typically in apartment complexes were always overcrowded and skilled guest workers from abroad lived in inhumane conditions.

John Miano, a lawyer and Founder of The Programmer's Guild, was the first to open the Pandora box, regarding the Prevailing Wage Rate discrepancies by petitioning employers and the same was first published in an article in the Computer World magazine in Washington DC, titled "H1-B Special Report". The first alarming loophole in the H1-B work visa program was first discovered in the year 2004. I was cited in the article as one of the H1-B victims affected by these discrepancies.

But then what was the loophole? Here is how the process worked –

Petitioning of a new H1-B visa application for an alien worker involved employer attestations (promises) prior to getting an approval from the Department of Labor. The Department of Labor looked at only two levels of the prospective workers eligibility based on the intended geographic location and the occupation of the worker. In simple terms, the Department of Labor will see only the occupation of the foreign worker and the location where the worker will work.

The amendments made to the prevailing wage rate information was important to justify that the foreign workers with needed skill sets were not available locally and were to be paid wages equal to or more than the local workers. But, the existence of multiple layers of body shops has created a grey market of many agents that 'broker' the intellectual capital of its foreign workers. It was therefore important to examine the main reason for guest workers working at wages lower in comparison to their American colleagues. It was important to justify that the companies were bypassing available local talent because manipulating the Prevailing Wage Rate Information gave them access to higher profits.

Back in 1993, CBS's *60 Minutes* television show aired a story on H1-B computer programmers who were contracted out to Hewlett-Packard for a mere $10 per hour, nowhere near what the company would have to pay the permanent residents.

So a question arises, are foreign workers desperate enough to want to work for such a low per hour rate and then pay taxes as well as a broker commission, when they can and want to be able to earn more? The answer hints at the alarming abuse of human rights of foreign workers that forces foreign workers to be seemly desperate for work.

You don't get paid for the hour. You get paid for the value you bring to the hour..

Let us examine the loophole whereby the employers could *legally circumvent not paying* the promised wage level first and then go on to understanding what makes the foreign workers ready to do work at *any* wage offered.

An American firm in the temporary staffing business, petitions for a work visa for a citizen from abroad, promising a monthly salary based on the prevailing wage rate of the location of work. The wage is determined on many factors. For now, let's just say there are two levels that are determined for a particular geographic location. The lowest (mean) or the highest (median) pay levels, which in simple terms means – An employer can choose to pay its employee, either the lowest or the highest pay or anything in between what is prevailing in that area.

The determination usually is made based on the educational qualifications, years of experience, location as well as the occupation of the foreign worker. Prior to August 2004, the only two levels of determining a prevailing wage were based on the workers Occupation and Location. The two more levels added were: Education and Experience. Since January 20,2010 , the wage database contains some valuable information other visa job databases do not have. Every record includes not only employer, job title, work location, industry, occupation, visa class, minimum wage, but also wage level, supervisory responsibility and education/training/experience/travel requirements.

H1-B Dependant Employers have conveniently used this Prevailing Wage Related Information to manipulate corporate profits, by finding this loophole in the Department of Labor standards.

Let's examine this with an example:

The Labor Condition Application (LCA) claims that the prevailing wage for a Systems Analyst in Charlotte North Carolina according to the Department of Labor's data in the fiscal year 2002 was $42,246. This wage is the Level 1 wage, which in most common terms, the wage paid for a less experienced entry-level technology worker

The Level 2 wage, for the experienced worker, one with higher education, generally with a Master's Degree and above and/or a few years of experience, the wage was $69,618 and the mean wage was $60,150. (The mean wage is an interim wage determination. This wage parity determination works as a neutral wage determination when accurate wage levels are not made).

Over and above, visa sponsoring employers were allowed to pay 95% of the claimed prevailing wage. So here, the employer is paying the H1-B workers the absolute lowest wage it can get away with, right down to the last penny, but *selling the same worker to the client at the highest allowed prevailing wage rate.*

Thus, by selecting the entry-level wage as the prevailing wage, the employer has about $18,000 in wage savings, but actually pocket the $18,000 because the 'brokers' sell the foreign workers to their clients at the highest allowed prevailing wage rate.

To explain this further, someone with a combination of an advanced degree and/or a couple of years experience, should be on the highest wage level 2, and get paid $69,618, is rather getting paid the same as an entry-level (Level 1) worker $42,246.

Note – Recent graduate students employed with large corporations with off shore training in India, and those with ready work visas (sitting overseas), are thus replacing experienced and existing H1-B visa holders, and by passing them as well as the local citizens. The growing numbers of those on visa status limbo, therefore is at large and hence a big concern. 'Stapling' of Green Cards to International Students, therefore may be an inadequate reform proposal *before* the 'brokerage' element is curbed.

While during the filing of the LCA petition for prospective H1-B worker, the mean wage was in fact $60,150. However, the employer uses his own survey determination to arrive at the Prevailing Wage, and hence pays the Level I wage.

Therefore, it will be important to inspect, that for every sponsored work visa, earns its visa sponsoring employer a hefty sum typically in the range of 15,000 to 30,000 US Dollars each month by virtue of simply brokering the talent gap. This hefty amount which otherwise would go directly to the citizens from abroad on guest worker visas allowing them to be at par with their American colleagues.

Could the work visa therefore, be a convenient way, for the earned income to stay within the country by virtue of the brokerage of intellectual capital?

Please note that the example presented of a foreign worker getting paid a measly $10 per hour at HP, was dated back in 1993, but the explanation of the prevailing wage rate was presented using data from the year 2002. The system was abused for almost 12 years, even when corporations were asking for an increase in the visa quota.

Building awareness

These issues got the required attention eventually. Take for instance, the case of the company Pacific West, in Iowa. The state of Iowa has very low living index as compared to other states such as California or New York City. Pacific West was headquartered in suburban Urbandale, in Iowa's capital city of Des Moines. Their two executives, Vishnu Reddy and Chockalingam Palaniappan were charged with filing false documents with the US Citizenship and Immigration Services and US Labor Dept. to take advantage of the lower wage requirements in Iowa.

A IT consulting firm that employs both US and H1-B visa workers from overseas. It is there, in a nondescript six-story office building at 2600 Aurora Ave., that dozens of skilled workers, mostly from India, were supposed to be working in 2004 and 2005.

But according to a federal lawsuit filed on Dec. 16, 2007 in the US District Court for the Southern District of Iowa, some of those who came to work for Pacific West didn't get to enjoy the town's charms, or the computer programming or engineering jobs they expected to fill., instead the workers were found working on the East and West coasts, and were found working for companies that had nothing to do with technology.

A federal investigation reveled that the allegations made against Pacific West as well as 4 other companies from Iowa investigated were part of a specific scheme that allegedly allowed employers to fraudulently cheat H1-B visa workers of their proper wage rates. Even though lawsuits have been brought against a few companies for H1-B visa fraud in the past, but allegations against Pacific West and other Iowa-based companies suggested to what may have become a common scheme to underpay H1-B visa workers by misrepresenting their geographic work location.

When the details of this alleged fraud emerged, 13 people in six states were arrested in connection with five IT services companies. And one company, named Vision Systems Group, was found guilty of fraud. The same company, that cost Akhil; a member of my organization his 4000$ and being debarred from applying for a US visa for 3 years.

Vision Systems Group was ordered to forfeit $7.4 million that it allegedly obtained through fraudulent means. Three other technology companies - Worldwide Software Services and Sana Systems, both based in Clinton, Iowa; and VenuriSoft of Clive, Iowa were further investigated for document fraud..

To read the allegations in the federal lawsuit, it sounds as though some companies used the H1-B program as a way to arbitrage low-wage rates in parts of the U.S., such as the Midwest, against labor shortages in higher-pay states. Acting as a response to received tips that companies in Iowa were inflating the numbers of workers employed at local offices in their state and US filings. Upon investigating the five companies involved, it was found that supposedly high-skilled tech workers bound for Iowa on H1-B visa often ended working in another state, sometimes for a third-party company and other times for an entirely different type of business such as a fast-food restaurant or a gas station.

The prevailing wage in Iowa could give employers a "30-40 per cent discount" on worker pay. According to court documents, Vishnu Reddy and Chockalingam Palaniappan falsely stated in federal and state visa petitions that H1-B visa workers whom they sponsored would be stationed at Urbandale from October 2004 through December 2008. But Pacific West allegedly did not have positions open to employ the workers.

In the case of Pacific West, Vishnu Reddy and Chockalingam Palaniappan were charged with one count of conspiracy to defraud the US and 11 counts of mail fraud.

The H1-B visa program was set up to help companies bring highly skilled workers into the US to fill jobs that they were having a hard time filling with American workers. Many agree that the program, which allows 85,000 skilled workers from overseas to enter the US each year, is fraught with examples of deceptive practices that result in visa workers getting paid less than what they should.

But what really hurt the image of foreign workers are the allegations that the work visa program systematically lets companies bring in lower-cost foreign labor when qualified US workers are available. The net effect is that tech wages in the U.S. are dampened, and job opportunities reduced for Americans.

There is also a flip side to the immigration policies that allows the brokerage of intellectual capital. The employer sanctions, that ignored the indentured servitude of its workers, have in fact created wealth in the nation where the talent was originally sourced from. What began as a convenience to fill the talent gap in a fragmented visa policy that refused to look at workers with dignity, has not only helped India become an outsourced hub creating employment opportunities, but has also helped in the infrastructure development as well. It has also created rich individuals that took the liberty of the indentured nature of the visa programs amassing huge personal wealth, and circumventing the cash flow, buying away chunks of land at a low price by virtue of 'cash deals'. The 'black money' campaign that takes away precious years from India's other political priorities, points at the need for both governments to look at a seamless integration of its human capital.

Besides the Outsourcing of visas, Outsourcing of jobs is the added convenience. To the corporate that can get work done for lesser costs to the company, a point of contact in both the countries were an excellent value proposition. How else can the birth of outsourcing be justified?

But for me, getting a job was easy. I found a job quickly online. It took just 48 hours to receive job offers. And to my surprise, AT&T, in New Jersey was one of them. Edison, Princeton, AT&T – the stories, linked to these places were heard a zillion times growing up. I was envy to most of my friends, who had arrived in The Americas before me, and were struggling to find a job.

As I cleared the interview for the position of a Data Analyst, I was faced with a challenge. I had to look for a company that could sponsor me an H1-B visa, requiring me to transfer my existing H1-B visa from my previous employer. And I had less than 45 days to find an employer, file the transfer and begin receiving my first pay check, else risk being in visa status limbo. I had to look for a company that would take part of my pay check in exchange for my being legally indentured to them by allowing them to be my H1-B visa sponsor.

The H1-B visa program is a temporary work visa program that permits employment of highly-skilled workers, but is also 'dual intent' in nature, which simply means that a foreign worker has two options. One option is to return back to their home country after the completion of their work. The other is to receive the benefit of a permanent residency (the 'green card'), if the employer files a petition on the workers behalf to be permanently employed with them.

This 'good faith' intent of the US Congress, via making available the option for a foreign worker to a permanent residency status, was an incentive for the foreign workers to outperform others, thereby creating a competitive labor market.

Unfortunately, because the H1-B visas are tied to employment, which means that an H1-B visa becomes invalid if the worker loses his job, has led to a wide spread grey market, in which the labor contractors use the 'carrot and stick' approach, creating an indentured workforce.

An explanation of the exploitative nature of the visa program is best understood by knowing that the H1-B visas are valid for up to three years and can be renewed once more only for an additional three years. While employed, it is relatively easy for a worker on an H1-B visa to transfer the visa to another employer. The transfers do not extend the time limit on the original visa. However, if the previous employer has filed a petition seeking a permanent residency status to its worker, changing employer would require initiating the process of filing for residency afresh. Visa shunting therefore is the greatest threat faced by the foreign workers.

Arrangement with the visa sponsor was like paying 'blood money' to a broker. My work visa too was bound to a visa sponsor employer. And that meant, giving away a large chunk of my salary to the company only because they were supposed to own me a visa. But that was a small price to pay, considering the freedom of being a permanent employee with AT&T soon, and a consequent Green Card. An interim second job to compliment the loss of income was therefore an alternative to be considered.

When the AT&T technical manager qualified me and made me a job offer, that included the amount I'd get paid per hour, I then had to go in search of a company that would agree to take me on board as an employee that will then outsource me, legally on paper, to the end client - AT&T. And for this, I had to part away a percentage of my hourly wage. AT&T would not sponsor my work visa direct.

With less time in hand, I zeroed in on a specific company that offered me the best possible 'rate'. We agreed on a 70:30 split. In simple terms, I had to pay 30% of the 84$ every hour I earned to the company that owned my H1-B work visa, just so they could 'officially' place me to work at 'their' customer location in AT&T. Out of the 30% that I part with, the company would pay one half of the medical insurance premium for me and my family as the group premiums was a lot cheaper. Insurance in the state of New Jersey for a family of two adults and one infant was approximately 800$ per month then. It was decided, company would pay half amount towards the monthly premium and the other half was to be deducted from my pay check every month.

So here is what I'd be left with – AT&T would be paying me 84$ for every hour worked. That is 13,440 $ per month.(normal working hours). Out of which, 30% or $25.20 cents of every hour worked would go to the company for holding my work visa, without which AT&T would not hire me. That is 4,032 $ monthly would go to the company while I keep the balance of 9,408$. I was not to be paid for any overtime. And I had to contribute 400$ additionally every month towards the medical insurance premium. Leaving me with 9,008$. But I also had 24% deductions towards federal and state taxes just like everyone else irrespective of their visa status. $3,225.60 cents was what I had to pay the government to be working in the country. So basically, I was left with 5,782.40$ every month, still a fair amount for a family of two adults and an infant. I was at a tremendous loss of $ 7,657.60 cents every month only because I was a foreign worker. I had regular tax deductions at source, but as a foreign worker I could never imagine receiving the benefits such as unemployment insurance, what my American colleagues eventually receive. In short, I earned $161,280.00 $, but I gave away $91,164.00 annually.

I was in for a rude shock, but this was the best offer I received, amongst the many I spoke with. The job was long term and permanent. My probation period was for one year, after which I could be a permanent employee of AT&T and get my Green Card sponsored. My wife was looking forward to arrive with our new born and working for AT&T was a once in a lifetime opportunity, that I did not want to miss.

So here I was, in my second job, with a steady pay, and with two employers to report to. I felt great. As long as I did my job well, I had nothing to worry about. Even though the visa sponsor owned my visa, I thought I was still in control, as I was the one working, and the one bringing in the moolah to the company. Honestly, I was on top of the world.

Dad was most happy to hear the news. Being a Nuclear Scientist himself, it was a pride to be working with AT&T. I could imagine him boasting with his colleagues at work. I never told him of the broker deal, because it didn't matter. What I earned in the United States, was still well over 2 lakh rupees per month, something that is next to impossible at my age and experience. Sujata had indeed brought about the change in my life. Gifts and letters from in-laws were most encouraging.

Little did I know then, the real test of acceptance was superficial! What lay in front of me was a crude fact of mishaps and career accidents that will leave me devastated and betrayed.

2 TWELVE YEARS A SLAVE

Belleville, in French literally meant, "a beautiful town". It was a quaint township, some 12 miles east of the Newark International airport and just 22 miles from New York City. Separated by the Hudson River, the township was nestled in a valley. Famous for its Japanese cherry blossoms, that bloom just two weeks in a year, the township was also a tourist destination to many. Watching many a Hollywood movies shot in the picturesque township we lived in, was always a delight. Adequate public transport, was an added advantage, we had, especially since Sujata didn't have a drivers license. Living in Belleville, was very peaceful. We knew quite a few families here and we socialized quiet a bit too. From the bank staff to super market employees, ours were not just known faces; our daughter was the special attraction to many. Lazy late Sunday morning brunch at the local Italian Diner was almost a routine. It gave Sujata a day off her household chores, allowing us the quality family time. The pair of bright yellow Canaries at home was in fact a gift to our daughter from the elderly Italian couple that owned this diner. Belleville had indeed been our home town - for close to 8 years.

My work place was 58 miles away, the second last exit on the Inter-State, before entering the state of Pennsylvania. But it was an easy commute considering driving on the opposite direction of the daily rush hour traffic heading into New York City. An hour of yoga, followed by a ready breakfast, I was in my driver's seat by 8 am. Life was a routine. As we settled down in our new lifestyle, we enjoyed our weekend trips to destinations that included out of state trips, making our summers memorable. Our trips extended to the nearby states of Pennsylvania, Virginia, Delaware, Maryland, Washington DC, Vermont, Upstate New York.

As our popularity of being 'settled' increased our value proposition with our families back home, we had regular visitors – including distant friends of distant relatives. We hosted the well known as well as the lesser known friends of friends of in-laws that included pilots, air line crews, and cine artists including a handful of India's leading super stars, arriving for a few days to a few weeks into the tri-state to perform as performing artists or on a business trip. We always had room for our guests in our three bedroom apartment. Our close proximity to the airport, offered a perfect vantage point serving as a free room and board, or the occasional store house for items shipped to us for the forthcoming signature events, hosted on behalf of the leading stars of bollywood.

Though the challenges of being in a foreign land on temporary short term visas were still unknown, we stood tall with being accepted by our families finally. Life was good, and we tried to make the best of what life threw at us.

It was a long winter day at work in Bedminster, New Jersey. I had already put in 54 hours in office that week, and today was Friday. As I hurriedly logged out of my workstation, it was already 6:50 pm. And I had a 58 mile drive back to the closest train station to catch the train into New York City to my second job. I was an IT instructor with a software training school on 23rd and Park Avenue, in Manhattan, New York City.

Like most immigrants, I too was industrious and hard working. And my family meant the world to me. It was a struggle, yet promised a wonderfully rewarding future. A beautiful wife and a gorgeous little princess to return to, exhausted from work, was worth it all. And like many guest workers in the United States, I also had two employers. One that owned my work visa and the other where I actually went into work every day. My visa sponsoring company too was owned by an Indian husband – wife team.

Soon, we would move closer to office in the quaint Bedminster

Township, away from the hustle of the city life. No more late hours at work, no more second job 80 miles away three days a week. And like most of my colleagues, I too would be home early. Take hot air balloon rides in the summer, enjoy barbeque weekends with friends. Eventually own a house, with white pickets' fences and colorful wild flowers in our beautiful garden. The thoughts were stimulating.

As I shifted gear of my new Honda SUV on the Interstate, there was already a snow flurry and the weather forecast on the radio predicted a snow storm. On most occasions, the drive on the interstate was pleasant. It gave me the opportunity to be calm and to think.

Tonight was different. Tonight there was a storm inside the car too. I was raging with anger. I had received the pink slip today. I was replaced by a new arrival from India that was willing to work for an even lower salary. To make it worst, he was a recent engineering grad, with just six months of in house training in India. His real hands on job would be the one he was replacing me with. Tonight I felt used and abused and I was eventually crying.

A week ago, I had asked my visa sponsor employer for a salary review which was way overdue - more than the promised six months. Today, I was fired.

I soon learnt that this was a common practice with Indian owned consulting firms. But I didn't think this would happen to me. I had searched and qualified for the job on my own. In essence, I had done my visa sponsor employer a favor, by qualifying them to be an approved vendor of the client. Besides, I had studied in the country, had over seven years of work experience in my field and most importantly, my client manager was even satisfied with my work.

As per the law, any visa sponsor employer can terminate a guest worker employee at will, simply by issuing a termination letter. It is upon the worker, on the employer dependant work visa, to look for another job, within a stipulated time frame of not more than 45 days. Failure to get a job, the visa status is deemed 'out of status', but the worker is not illegal, to get back on a legal visa status, the worker needs to produce a pay slip and often pay for their own visa fees and receive approval of a new work visa petition. Also, a foreign worker can only work for the employer that has petitioned the visa.

A good friend Venu Gopal, originally from Hyderabad has an interesting story. Venu has a Master's degree in Mathematics. A loving husband and a father of two, he is one of the sad statistics of the exploitative indentured nature of the H1-B visa system. An Oracle developer, he had been on the H1-B visa for three years. He had worked with the big names in and around the tri state. In between projects, he often would fall back upon the bench salary. At one point of time, there were approximately 300 H1-B workers like him on his body shops payroll. When the projects dried, Venu was unable to receive the promised salary while he searched for a new assignment. With three dependants and no salary, it was important for him to move closer into the cities where cash work was easily available as in intern break from work. He moved into New Jersey with his family, and worked at a gas station, giving telephone interviews on the side. Unfortunately for him, when he did get the job offer, he did not have a pay stub to prove his being in continuing legal status. And as such his H1-B transfer was declined. Quiet and warm natured Venu worked at the gas station, under the table, for the next four years, before returning back to India with his family; just in time for his children's primary school admissions.

Professor Ron Hira, in his briefing paper has rightly said – "It is clear from the data that many, if not most, of the top H1-B and L-1 employers do not use the visa programs as a bridge to permanent immigration. These visa programs are being used in substantial ways simply for temporary labor."

From October 1, 2013 to June 30, 2014, U.S. employers filed 418,429 labor condition applications for H1-B visa jobs, out of which; 9,548 were denied, and 12,724 were withdrawn. During the same time, the Department of Labor made decisions on 54,242 labor certifications for employment based green card: 3,983 were denied, and 2,982 were withdrawn. This goes to prove yet again, that the H1-B visa is mainly used for labor mobility!

Employer's petitioning to hire foreign workers, must also promise to continue to pay a salary to their 'benched' workers, but, often employers do not. And that's what happened to me too! Like Venu, and many others, I too was nothing more than a commodity to my body shop. We were products of a system, products that you use and then throw away. The law allowed a visa sponsor employer to be in safe harbor by simply offering a termination letter to its foreign employee. My visa sponsor threatened me with a termination. But I wasn't worried. Thankfully, I continued my teaching second job and focused on looking for a full time job that would help me be in legal immigration status.

Because the work visa laws were employer centric in nature, agencies, also loosely termed as 'body shops', 'sweat shops' even "chop shops', violated contractual agreements with impunity.

Just half a month ago, I had rushed my wife to a hospital in a medical emergency. It wasn't until the next morning, when I was informed of the lapse in our medical insurance. My body shop simply had not paid the required premium fees towards our medical insurance despite my pay slip showing regular deductions during the entire 11 months that I was employed and working with AT&T. Like a fool I paid my employer 400$ every month, never knowing where the money went.

Even though there was enough evidence to report abuse, I did not know whom to approach for help. The body shop had threatened me with dire consequences, and of having me deported. Back then, the Department of Labor approved the applications of employers petitioning for foreign workers; and did not have information available for the guest workers regarding reporting abuse, there also weren't any whistleblower provisions for foreign workers that encouraged reporting of abuse against their employers; needlessly the police too could not be approached as it was unclear if the issues specific to individuals on specific work visas, were understood, or fell under the purview of the local police because, as I later found out, *work visas for skills not available locally* itself were unknown then.

As the letters and calls from the collection agencies became frequent, I settled to pay $3,800 to the hospital and had the balance written off as charity … Here I was – a foreign *guest worker*, that has a US education, that managed to get not one but two employers, earned a decent livelihood, managed a family, made honest contributions every pay check, paid my taxes just like American citizens… and had to be thrown into charity when my family was in need. If this wasn't enough, three days later, I received a fed ex, containing an official termination letter from my employer.

The H1-B visa laws state that an H1-B visa holder cannot stay legally without a pay check for more than 30 days. And I had only three weeks left, to find a job or risk being out of visa status. To many people being without a job was difficult especially when there were family members that depended on it. Without a visa, that was tied to a job, was even more precarious. I risked the conditional agreement with the state and the federal governments of being in lawful visa status.

It was time to negotiate. My visa sponsor was expecting my phone call, and an in person meeting was confirmed. We struck a deal -- I had to pay him cash to receive a payroll check with a 30% mark up. In actual numbers, I had to pay 1150 $ every 2 weeks to receive a payroll check of 800 $, the bare minimum to stay legally within the immigration boundaries.

The understanding was cruel but with no way out, it was the only one. I had to exchange cash in return of a payroll check. And I had to pay a 30% commission to receive the company check, just so I can prove I was receiving regular salary and therefore in legal visa status. In essence I was paying the 30% mark up – 350$ every 2 weeks ($700 a month) to keep me in legal visa status, and the worst of it all, *I was actually compelled to commit fraud not to the government alone, but to the society that was also my home!!!*

The approaching threat of the dot com bust, depleting savings, recent sickness of my family and the coming winter, I was worried. It had been 2 months, since I had last exchanged cash for the payroll check and so I was out of visa status. I was fanatically looking for a job.

Thankfully I qualified for a position with Intel Corporation at Folsom, California. I was offered a position as a Senior Web Architect, and that too as a direct employee. Finally, a permanent job meant getting out of the wrangle of the visa sponsor brokers. No more visa shunting or getting fleeced by them. But, this dream too was unfulfilled. The broker company that held my visa sought a headhunter finder's fee from the Intel HR personnel towards the cost of training and maintaining me. So the job offer was revoked simply because the visa sponsor broker's demand for a fee was in fact to release me.

To make it worse, the employer simply refused to exchange my cash for a payroll check that was required to show that I was in legal visa status, afraid that I might jump his company and with the pay stub apply for a visa transfer towards an H1-B visa from Intel. The position from Intel was filled shortly and I lost yet another opportunity.

Dejected and frustrated, I opted for another visa sponsor that could help me stay in legal status. Someone that could take the risk of filing my H1-B transfer, without the pay stubs required as proof of being in legal status. I however, had to pay 1800$ - attorney's fees as well as the visa filing fees. Should the visa approval come through, half of the paid amount would be reimbursed after serving three months with the company.

When you're desperate, you make do with anything offered and that's what I did. It was the beginning of July already, and I had spent the entire summer looking for a job. Negotiating, hoping, praying... Through it all, the bills continued, and all that was left of our savings were low four figures and steadily dropping.

In about a fortnight, I received a phone call offering me a position of an Information Architect, with Merrill Lynch at the North Tower of the World Trade Center in New York City. I qualified, yet again. The petition to transfer the visa status was filed and I begun work immediately. I couldn't get paid until the petition transfer was approved, and so worked for almost six weeks without pay, and without the knowledge of my manager at Merrill Lynch. The market had slumped and the dot com bubble had finally burst. Many friends including those who were American citizens were jobless. But I was thankful to have a job to go to. Six weeks without a pay, at a time when the bills were overdue, and a serious need for medical treatment for my wife, it was once again a relief.

One afternoon, my 5th day at work, with my new job at Merrill Lynch, my wife called from a pay phone informing me that the utilities in our apartment had been shut off. Earlier, both our telephones had been shut off due to nonpayment of bills. We were behind our rent by 2 months and the going was tough. Hoping and praying for the visa transfer to arrive early. I was afraid to ask for an cash advance from my visa sponsor employer and tell him of my challenges for the fear of being taken advantage of once again. So we spend the night without heat or electricity, cooking on the summer's left over barbeque candles that were kept stored in the basement.

Sujata's quirks come at the precise moment, something that is her inherent quality. That night as we put on extra warm clothes and huddled together wishing good night, Sujata's words put us all three into a roaring laughter. She simply said – "damn ... winter is early this year. Who will hug me to keep me warm tonight?"

In the well to do nonresident Indian community, we were a penniless family and we had hesitated in seeking help. The next morning, for the first time I borrowed money from Venu, who himself was struggling at a job in a gas station nearby. With the borrowed money, and a promise to pay back with an interest, we paid the pending telephone bills, restored electricity and gas in our apartment, and had 300$ left until the pay check arrived – an accumulated take home pay check – minus the brokerage was going to be 9,300 $. !!! The late fees on our car payment were acceptable to us and we decided to pay off the balance amount as soon as we received the money. A car in the severe winter months was not a luxury, it was a necessity.

It was already 48 days since the petition filing receipt was received. And I was hoping to receive the approved petition anytime. The atmosphere at home, that night was blissful. We didn't speak much, but had a quiet dinner watching an Indian movie. Our daughter sensing the less stressful atmosphere was a gleeful jumping jack that night. The spirit of happiness was back again and I felt at ease knowing the crisis has finally ended.

As we sat huddled on our couch, watching the movie…I received a text message – "The Petition number EAD 1440132*** has been approved". I leaped with joy. Today indeed was a lucky day. Sujata was in tears and ran inside the kitchen. I followed her inside and hugged her warmly. We both wept.

Over the past couple of weeks, Sujata too had taken up a job. In spite of her having a US education, she worked as a counter sales girl in a gift shop at a mall and got paid under the table only because we did not have the time or the money to pay for her visa transfer from the dependant spouse visa to a new H1-B visa. Her job required long hours of standing, frequent lifting of heavy card board boxes containing the store's inventory. The job had taken its toll on her health. She was only 36 with a prolapsed uterus. Her back hurt and she was in constant pain. A setback, yet she continued and fought back tirelessly.

The past couple of months of unwarranted crisis had brought us closer. I learnt a lot about her in those few hours that we got to spent together. Today the crisis was over. We hugged. We wept and we prayed. It was the closest, most intimate moment for us.

I distinctly remember, it was a Friday when we received the text message informing us of the H1-B petition transfer approval. That meant the pay check would be a fat one in another 2 weeks! I could start all over and buy medical insurance for my wife's falling health. Afraid to commit this time, I also secretly planned a winter vacation for us, during Christmas holidays as a surprise. Enthusiasm at home was at its peak. And the coming Christmas would promise to be a wonderful one. For now, I was glad she was not working and was at home resting.

Autumn was ending. The trees in our backyard of our three bedroom apartment were beginning to shed their leaves. It was that time of the year, when the sun and late-year rain played hide n seek. The coming winter was welcome as we would be confined to our apartment. And need to go out less.. and spend less. Blame the weather and be thrifty. Honestly…. I was happy!

Because, the recession that followed after the dot com bubble burst, many American workers as well as the foreign guest workers were jobless. Though the American workers had their social security and other welfare assistance from the government to fall upon, the foreign guest workers, especially those with a body shopper, simply had no choice but to return back to their native country or find immediate work – even jobs that paid under the table.

This also was the time, following the 9/11 incident. The heavy scrutiny on any brown skinned individuals took its toll on many.

There were some workers, like me, who had lost their jobs and colleagues within the rubbles of the Ground Zero. The American government disbursed financial aid to those affected, through its Federal Emergency Medical Aid program. Many took the benefits, some the disadvantage. Interestingly, many companies that had subcontracted H1-B workers to companies in the World Trade Center, made claims seeking the FEMA aid, however, none of the H1-B workers received any benefit; needlessly my visa sponsor denied me the right to my salary, stating his inability to raise an invoice towards my time worked. The salary of the past couple of weeks never came through.

What was heard in this heated argument however was – "Show me the signed time sheets submitted and I will gladly pay you. If you harass me, I will be forced to put the law onto you. You do not want that to happen to you…not at this time, do you? Where will your family go if you are in jail? "

How was I to produce the signed time sheets from my manager that were buried in the building rubbles of the World Trade Centre? I had even lost my laptop.

I was just two working days or in the literal sense, 16 hours away from receiving my salary that included my back wages of $9,300. I pleaded with my employer, but only to receive his bigger threats and verbal abuses. With less than 150$ left, this pay check could have put us through the winter, despite being out of work. My wife's failing health was of utmost priority.

They say, life puts us through challenging times to test our strengths. It puts us through the downside just so as to remind us of his existence. It was a test of faith. It had been six months already since we have had the hovering dark clouds above us, with an occasional ray of sunshine, only to be washed all away by the cold wet darkness again. But little did I realize then, the real journey of our lives had just begun. Our fate had been defined by our impulses to the events around us. But, I was changing, in response to the outward changes that affected our lives.

To say of destiny as something that happens only to me, is to assume that in essence I always remain the same, changeless at the core, amid the limitless unending changes of life and history.

Unknown to us then, a new destination was slowly opening up that would give us a new identity. And the only way to be fully identified would be by a story – of the kind only God could tell – Of the unfolding of life in all its depths and complexities. Making a deeply intimate connect with the self. I was to find my destiny. The events over the next few days were to have a profound impact on our lives, those that will vigorously shake our core belief system, making a deep impact that will be permanent and long lasting.

3 BANGED UP ON CHRISTMAS

It was 8:30 pm on a Saturday. I drove down to the local Seven Eleven for a gallon of milk. The store was hardly a distance from my apartment, but the nasty winter chill forced me to drive down wearing just a winter jacket over my cotton overalls.

As I pull out of the driveway, I noticed being followed by a squad car. Within minutes, I am asked to pull over, the flashing lights draining the street lights. As the police officer, inspects my license, I am asked to step out of the car and quickly handcuffed. No reading of my rights. No explanation. I was simply handcuffed and shoved into the back seat.

Back in the precinct, I have my mug shot taken and am shoved into a mini cell that was not more than 7 feet by 5 feet. I still had no idea what could be the reason for my being locked up. I was waiting for answers. And I was all by myself in the cell. I was shaking terribly and crying.

"You are allowed one phone call" said a police officer upon entering the holding cell. He continued, "Make sure who ever you call, bring the $200 bail money or you'll end here until Monday when the court opens".

It is 11:30 in the night, when my friend came with the bail money and I was released. I had been in the cell for close to two hours. And it has been over three hour's since I left home. I knew my wife would be worried. And I was worried too; I needed to get out of the jail as soon as I could. This definitely was a serious threat. More importantly, I worried for the safety of my wife and daughter. Being on the dependant spouse H-4 visa, she did not own a driving license, nor did she have a bank account. I was all that she had, in a foreign country. And worst still, we had a small daughter.

"Be present in the court at 9 am Monday. Be there or else we will come and get you" ordered the officer behind the desk as I took receipt of the bail money. "Sure I will sir, but if I could simply know the reason to be here tonight?" – I asked. The answer simply took me back. "You were caught driving a vehicle with a suspended license. You had the nerve to drive around, when your license had been suspended for 3 months! "

As I narrated the ordeal to my friend on my way back in his car, it was clear that I was a victim of being scrutinized as a suspect due to my ethnic origin. Post 9/11, this was very common throughout the United States of America's.

It was almost daylight when I went to bed. I had spent the night, going through the events of the past few months. I spent thinking of the reasons to the continued mishaps in our life and tried to find answers. Most of all, for the first time in 10 years in America, I was confronted for the safety of my family. I was in a crisis and I needed urgent help.

The 2 hours spent in jail was humiliating and I was hurting deeply. It was time to stop the negative events happening in my life and to take action. It was a personal attack on my self esteem and my pride. I wanted to share but I couldn't. It was at 5 am (Eastern), that I finally decided to make the call.

I must have slept for two maybe three hours, when our door bell rang. A middle aged, Caucasian gentleman, with salt n pepper hair in blue jeans and a brown leather jacket introduced himself producing his identification. Despite the lack of sleep, I observed that there was something extraordinary about this gentleman. The way he spoke with finesse, his constant smile, his body language or maybe it was his name – I was in a comfort zone immediately. We drove around in his car, visiting the place of the incidence; the police impound lot as well as the precinct, as I narrated him my story. All he did was listen patiently, take pictures – of me, of my passport, my valid visa, and my valid driver's license.

Who was this person that came knocking on my door on an early Sunday morning, wanting to know what really happened?? He definitely did not seem hostile, as I was so very used to. Could he be the person that sat all along in the government vehicle parked yards away from our apartment building? Whoever he was, he was indeed a great soul. Less than an hour with him, and all worries seemed to have dissolved…Before I could get to know more about him, he left! As swiftly as he had come in his dark black van with dark tainted windows!

It wasn't until late that night, did I know more about my morning visitor. He was Norman Lono, an ace photographer and a photo journalist with the 'USA Today'. He had also been on ground the desert storm. He had won a couple of awards too, a Google search revealed.

My wife had no idea whatsoever of my most recent adventures. And I hoped to keep it that way. I always shared my deepest secrets with her and sought her advice. She was after all a friend first. This time, I was too scared to scare her. I prayed and hoped she could never get to know about the incident, not even when there were two full pages narrating the incident in the nation's largest circulating newspaper – The 'USA Today'.

Monday morning, I leave home early. To my wife, it was in the pursuit of a job interview. In reality, I was walking in the cold, heading towards the court house. A 40 minute walk in the blistering cold. Most of the court appearances throughout the 4 months were swift and did not take more than an hour each time. Every court hearing, I was early and sat in the front row, maintaining direct eye contact with the presiding judge. Even though the court appearances were less frequent, as the winter snow approached, I was on time, every time.

I could not afford a lawyer. I didn't have the money, but even if I did, I would never know whom to approach. Honestly, I did not even know, if foreigners like me on temporary work visas could even qualify to hire a lawyer. If I knew, I would have hired one to go after the notorious body shops that fleeced me first. This was all new to me. So I was represented by a lawyer, appointed by the courts.

In the months that followed, I was proved to be not guilty and had my driving license restored. The freedom gained at the end of the soon to come horrendous months ahead, had no meaning left, compared to what I would soon be losing forever.

Christmas was around the corner, and I had a reason to make this a best Christmas ever. Our daughter was growing up and we wanted her to know and to understand the spirit of Christmas. Pranauti, our four year old, whom we would lovingly call 'Cookie', needed to understand the meaning of why we celebrate Christmas, just as we celebrated Diwali. This year, the Christmas tree was large. It was about seven feet tall. Adorned with decorations, and cascading rows of tiny flashing multi colored lights. The lights jumped and dimmed in sync with the rhythm of the Christmas carols. The red stockings lay over the fire place next to the tree, and with the room lights turned off, the tree looked heavenly. The entire household was spiritual.

As Sujata walked in the living room, with a glass of milk and cookies for Santa, I was in my rocking arm chair with Cookie on my lap. As we look at the milk glass and cookies placed, I warmly hug my daughter closely and say out loud – "Don't you go near that now, I don't want Santa to take away my cookie by mistake". As she hugged me tightly, she said – "You are my Santa, dadda"

Little did I know then, this was going to be our last Christmas together.

The very next morning, the morning of December 25th, Bert, our neighbor across the street, a Filipino, calls me up to inform me that my parked car had been smashed with pieces of the car debris strewn on the street. As I inspect the vehicle, I realize the car had been hit from behind and was quiet a mess. It would cost me a good deal to get it fixed. The police report said it was a hit and run. Unfortunately, my insurance company refused to pay for the costs of the damages.

So here I was, two months behind the car payment, with a damaged rear side that would cost me at least $3000 to fix. No job, a pending court case, and drastically failing health of my wife with no medical insurance, a small daughter and no family back home to fall upon. What made it worst was, I knew I needed help, but I did not know whom to approach.

These events had a serious strain on my family life, compounded with Sujata's rapidly falling health. Sujata was spending most of her time lying on bed. There was a huge lump on her lower back and it was only getting bigger. I had a decision to make. I had to stay strong and come out of the crisis.

On my 10th Christmas Eve in the United States, I was confronted with the threats. Could this be yet another motive to drive us out of the white dominated community we were living in? There were no accidents in life, only signs. Could this recent event be yet another reason for us to look at life in greater detail? Would life be preparing us for something of a greater unknown? – What could get worse than the life in the present?

It was 2 in the afternoon. It was dark and gloomy outside. We had a snow fall throughout the night. And the slush of the passing vehicles outside could be distinctly heard.

As I sat quietly that afternoon, I knew I had to take action. And first seek for the safety of my family. I didn't want to leave the country without receiving justice of being wrongfully detained. Yet, I did not want to compromise on another attack on the security of my family.

With no money left whatsoever, the only option available was to head home. We had exhausted our options. Every incident took away a large chunk of my identity, of who I was proud to be. All that was left of me was the core of who I was – a head of the family with two innocent dependants. And I controlled their fate, because they were associated with mine. I was guilt ridden. I blamed myself for being responsible to having put my wife through these challenges consistently. I saw myself as a failure, not able to provide the basic of the needs.

Despite these hardships and the tremendous physical pain, Sujata refused to look at the option of going back to India – even for a short term. As I sit beside her on the bed clutching her hand in mine, she said - "Where will we stay? Who will give us shelter? None of our families have forgiven us. You know it well, if I go back to my family – I would never get to return to you? This is our home now, if we are to die here, it might as well be together"

Sujata, the youngest of her sibling grew up in a secure protective family. As in every successful migrant in a city of dreams, her family has gained the reputation and is very well known in the community, having influential connections right up to the cushiony seats of the state legislative.

That we were married, and living overseas was reason enough to have the social and emotional disconnect with our respective in laws. Returning back from the land of opportunity as failures where getting a visa itself was difficult to many, was insulting to our families. Families therefore would find the reasons to keep us separated from one another by virtue of us being economically unstable yet again. Sujata's reasoning was to caution me of the possible outcome based on our past experiences.

Having spent a decade in The Americas, I too didn't want to leave the country, even if for a short break, not without officially clearing my name in any case and I prayed that the court case would came to an end soon. Neither could I send them home, as we were unwanted by our families. We never shared our ordeals with them. And we kept the challenges to ourselves. It was freezing cold outside, and I couldn't drive because the case was pending. Sujata couldn't drive because her visa status would not allow her to hold a driver's license. And we had a small daughter, who had just begun her kinder garden. There was absolutely no money left and I was helpless. I buried my head on her chest and wept. I asked for her forgiveness.

31st of December is usually a day when people all around the world celebrate ushering the new years. As my wife lay helplessly in bed, I silently make a resolution and spring into action irrespective of the outcome. I jotted down a list of tasks for the next 24 hours, and sprang into action—without discussing it with my wife.

The next morning I watch the tow truck take away my Honda SUV. I gave up my car even though I knew it would show up as a repossessed vehicle – a negative remark on my credit report.

I called upon my school friend in California seeking his help, explaining to him the ordeal of the last few months, the recent court case and wife's failing health. With his help, I purchased two confirmed one way tickets to India for my wife and daughter.- flying over Paris. A brief stopover in transit at Paris would be the least I could do for her, on her last visit out of the United States of America.

On Jan 28th, 2002, my family were safe and finally out of the Americas and had arrived into India allowing me to fully focus on the pending court case. On the final court date of March 12th, my birthday, I was ruled 'not guilty' of the charges levied.

Was it the continuous stress and mental exhaustion, or the poor nutrition, I was suffering bouts of cough and high fever since 2 weeks. With no medical insurance, soon enough, I too made my way to India only to be admitted into a hospital upon arrival; I now owed a total of about $7,000 to friends... all borrowed in the last four months.

4 BEING A FOREIGNER HOME

I was returning to India after a gap of 5 plus years. India had its own set of perception of the returning Non Resident Indians. Inadvertently I was scrutinized by all as I had been in the Indian news as well, of being a witness and a victim of 9/11. The Times Of India, had a special coverage on its page 3, highlighting my plight in the 9/11 aftermath.

Since the last Sujata had seen of me - 40 days ago, I had lost weight from a healthy 86 kilos to a lean 42 kilos. I had been in and out of the hospital ICU 3 times in a brief span of 4 months. I had been diagnosed with lung tuberculosis. And by now, I was coughing blood.

Being the black sheep of our respected families, we understood one another well. Our families had not interacted with one another since our marriage, and our presence in India, as failures, was a splendid opportunity for them to vent their barely-concealed disapproval. As families were gearing up for their agendas, Sujata did menial odd jobs near our house just so she could afford the daily 300 Rs worth of medicines for me, ignoring her own physical pain.

As my parents blamed their daughter-in-law for bringing the "bad luck" that caused my ill-health and our bad fortune, Her parents blamed me for being an inadequate nincompoop. Hidden grievances surfaced, and frequent accusations flew from both sides. As a result, formal complaints were registered against me with the local police by both the parties. While in-laws charged me with cruelty and harassment against my wife, my parents pressed charges accusing me and my wife of using our poverty as an excuse to claim their property—which included a huge mansion with 21 rooms, 16 of which were vacant.

My health had drastically fallen. I coughed blood chunks when I spoke for long. The heavy dosage of medicines made me drowsy and agitated due to lack of sleep. The weather was hot and there was no air conditioner. To add more to the agony, my parents asked us to leave their house stating it wasn't a free room and board anymore. We were accused of plotting to claim their property. But as we had stopped our daughter's education mid way and rushed back to India, it was imperative her schooling continued despite the losses we as parents incurred. I was agitated. I was frustrated. I was losing hope.

We were at a total loss, and as predicted the challenges were unending. It was time to let go, just so our daughter may have a good life. The consistent nags, and accusations at home were increasing. Caught in between the daughter in law – mother in law fights, I reached at a point of frustration when I slapped my wife in my fit of anger. What happened afterwards was obvious, both the families had a face to face confrontation, making it a public spectacle, when accusations flew wildly in the open in a public place – at a nearby temple garden.

Despite all their differences however, both families agreed, on one thing alone: I needed mental help. I was mentally stressed and advised 'mental treatment'. I was not consulted and without my will, I was admitted into a government mental asylum in Mumbai, where my hands and legs were tied up and I was threatened to be subject to electric shocks as treatment, all the while confined in a dark secluded room that had locked iron gates and a guard outside 24x7.

Because both families with their alter-egos were determined, I couldn't imagine, where I would be sent next from here. It was terrifying. As always is the case though, a bribe of a100 Rs for a minutes phone call greatly helped. I was released that same day after spending a week's detention in the mental hospital.

However, there was a hidden agenda behind this exercise. And, later did I understand, that it did serve the intended purpose that both our families had supposedly agreed upon. A week's detention was enough to be declared insane. The evidence produced declared me being insane at age 36, and hence no claimant to the parental property, while the same evidence was used to file a divorce petition in the family courts resulting in my official divorce decree judgment Unfortunately, a letter from the President of the Mumbai Psychiatric Association, stating my 'sound mind' was of no help, even when I moved an application in the family courts seeking visitation rights for my daughter.

Life was a paradox. That's what I learnt. While resistance to globalization was indeed the cultural differences, as I had witnessed in The Americas, I witnessed resistance for me being culturally different from my in-laws because I belonged to a different caste. And these cultural differences could simply be removed by me being financially secure – something which was best achieved by going back to The Americas. So basically, my unwillingness of returning back to The Americas was keeping me away from my daughter!!

A visa to any country is always a privilege, and in essence I have been fortunate. Ever since the age of 23, until today, I have always had in my possession a valid visa to the United States of America. Even though I had the compelling option of going back, I chose to stay back in India, in an attempt to reunite with my family and salvage my reputation. There was also the tuberculosis. In the United States I had no medical insurance; India was the only option available. And my own survival was at stake.

While our families sued and counter-sued one another, I found myself homeless with no place to go. I had no money whatsoever, and was estranged from my extended family because I couldn't care enough to provide for her, more so at a time when my health was failing and they feared my death, I was ostracized by my own cousins and relatives because I had the audacity to marry a woman from a different caste. I had nowhere to go. I lived as a homeless under the Mumbai-Pune expressway flyover bridge for almost a week, before the Swaminarayan ashram, adjacent to the Indian Institute Of Technology Campus at Powai, in Mumbai city was suggested.

A serene, spiritual and peaceful ashram, that became my home for nearly six months. The trip from the mental asylum to the ashram was sudden, and I was still reeling from it. Throughout the time I stayed in the ashram, it had been my comfort. It shielded me from the social judgment and the overwhelming noise of traffic in the city outside.

It gave me the time to be with myself. It was when here in the ashram, I received summons from the court. I had to make myself available for yet another 'fight for the right' in my own country. This time it were the family courts. I had to prove that I was not deported. I had to justify my failure (not my ability) in providing for my family. I had to justify "life on an H1-B program", I knew I was a victim of the laws that weren't meant to favor foreign workers, but American employers alone. I was abused, and I was hurting deeply inside. It was so very personal, that I had trouble communicating with anyone-- not even my wife, my closest friend.

The ashram, allowed me to reflect and recollect on life's events. It was here that I did accept that our hardships while in the United States on the student visas were easy, though strife with less money throughout our coursework. But our troubles began, with the H1-B program that prohibited us from seeking employment outside of the brokers. Repeated emotional abuse, and the humiliation faced by the employers, and my inability to do anything about it, had its consequences in the home front too. As I helplessly succumbed to the humiliation meted out by the employers, where in I was not paid even for the money that was rightfully mine – money for which I had toiled sweat and blood, I did not realize I was also loosing the respect of my wife.

In one of our arguments I remember her words distinctively –

"Bastard! You lied to me. You promised me the world. And here I am your slave. One day, I will take everything you own, separate you from your own child and then report you for gross neglect. Then you will understand what sacrifices I have made. You promised me the world, and this is the life you give me after 12 years?"

Her words had stung like the bee. The words were poison darts that pierced through the heart. Numbing at first, and then slowly bleeding itself to death. And that's exactly what happened to our marriage. - It irrevocably broke down.

Every layer of abuse from outside put a layer of discontent, increasing unhappiness between us. It was becoming evident that Sujata's threshold to sustain the abuse when she herself had limited mobility and freedom on the dependant visa had drastically fallen. On our return back to our own home country, in a secure familiar environment that comfort was once again threatened when accusations flew off the handle at home. When I had failed as a provider, and that I lived in an ashram, it was obvious she too had given up and lost all hopes of a life married with someone that was unable to care for self, lest his family.

When families were unwilling to listen and refused to understand what I had to say, it was therefore obvious, that I had lost all respect not only by her but also by families – to them failure was not an option.

While I went into oblivion in the ashram, living life as a vegetable, waking at odd hours with a scream reminding me of the 9/11 incident, and sleeping during the day – she decided to finally end the agony and filed in her divorce papers.

I had returned back 'home'. I had returned not only to a country where I was born, but to the same land where we, as parents, had chosen to travel to, for our daughter's birth. Living through the courtroom ordeal in New Jersey, I was to be present once again in the Mumbai court rooms.

However, unfortunate it may seem, but I was witnessing the judiciary system of world's two largest democracies, all within the span of a few months.

The family court rooms, in Mumbai, I am afraid to say, were a mockery of the Indian democracy. They are often referred to as the "anadi" courts – idiots courts. There is no decorum and there is no discipline whatsoever. The lawyers here rule. Period! There are more lawyers here than in any other court premises I have ever seen.

The court room where the judge presided over our case was a room not more than 500 sq ft, where private issues and matters between disputing couples were openly debated. The free for all public spectacle occurs right in front of others waiting to be called next. Though litigants are prohibited from entering into the room, their lawyers are often seen standing inside the court rooms, ogling, even when the presiding case is not represented by them, especially while the court proceedings are in session. It is a tremendously embarrassing situation to be standing there listening to other couples venting their emotions, with accusations that are both hilarious and embarrassing alike.

Unfortunately, ours too was one such sad experience. She had filed her divorce petition after living separate for more than almost a year. I had not seen her or the child since then. And it was a pleasant feeling to see her in the court. She looked much better than what I had seen her before she and the daughter were whisked away.

The court room was on the 5th floor and poorly lit. The elevators opened up directly on to the waiting room where litigants sat with sunken faces waiting to be called. A whiff of urine stench greeted you as soon as the elevator doors open up.

Just outside the elevators, to the right, a small metal desk and a chair with an old Reddington typewriter occupied the open windows of the 3 feet wide corridor. On the desk are a heap of papers and files. The bald stout man sitting on the desk is busy typing, making a loud irritating clicking with his typewriter. On numerous occasions, as I waited to be called, I have observed him patiently and had even been able to befriend him. I had been impressed by his dedicated efforts to serve the people. He was never found sitting alone, there always were people hovering around him, dictating their versions of matrimonial discord in local dialect, while he translated what is heard onto his own legal version with horrible broken English. Though not a court employee, he sits here to help litigants type their legal petitions! He never looks up, except when payments are collected. The forms are available for a rupee or two, but his costs are anywhere from 50 Rs to thousands. Nevertheless, he does a great service and is found accommodating regards payments as well. As I witnessed, when a destitute penniless village woman offered her gold ring as payment, he willingly accepted! Candidly, I was getting introduced to the world of corruption here.

The court room inside, itself could not be more than 500 sq feet, but there were approximately 20-25 people in the room, including the presiding judge, that sat on an elevated wooden floor by the windows. The ceiling fan looked old, just as the Reddington typewriter outside; and possibly were the ones left behind by the British. The floors as well as the walls were dirty.

The children's visitation room, two stairs below, was the biggest disappointment. It was a large dingy room, with broken toys scattering the floor, possibly from the previous day, and was still untidy. The walls here too, were dirtier than in the court room. The cob webs throughout the ceiling corners probably were left unattended, reminding us disputing parents never to lose their fight in seeking freedom of their children. On a wooden desk at the entrance of the room was a big ledger book where the name of the parent and the child is maintained before allowed a visit inside! Innocent children from broken families were forced to meet their parents here.

As I sit in silence, I felt sad acknowledging that children were subject to the same stigma as adults, even when they were innocent and torn between disputing parents. I wondered if the corporate social responsibility could be effectively utilized to add a little life to these dingy rooms where innocent children met their parents. Worst still, family courts did not make any attempts to counsel the children.

It wasn't difficult to me in making my decision. I will not be subjecting my child to these inhuman processes.

During most of the court appearances, Sujata's lawyer did all the talking. Even when she was questioned by the judge, all she ever said was – "Ask my lawyer!"

Her lawyer, the secretary of the bar council then, was also a close family friend of my in-laws. He was paid to fight. Often provoking me, he mocked at my present physical state, often teasing me of the torn shirt I wore, and at times, commenting on my slouching posture. He kept the court room alive with his loud voice and wise cracks. He was witty no doubt, and he didn't have to even try in making every one laugh, including myself. I thought of him as the jester in the court room. Overall it was a once in a lifetime experience, something so different from the courtroom I experienced in the United States.

It was surprising to see a person having such a contrasting behavior. Outside the court premises, her lawyer would be most friendly asking me to stay positive, but once inside he had a completely different provocative stance. This duality was unique, but I guess is a much required trait that linked directly with the profession he was in. I wondered if this could be the reason; lawyers are required to wear a black coat over a white shirt.

Throughout the eleven months, in the courtroom, as I choose to answer his allegations with a simple – "no comments, no contest" motion, he seemed frustrated and finally made an attempt to an out of court settlement. Standing outside by the parking lot, out of the courtroom premises, he tried his best, when he said – "Look, this is getting dragged endlessly and I am charging my client for every court session I represent her. So I am offering you an option. I have advised her not to get into the monthly maintenance headache, rather settle down to one lump sum amount from you, and then we can consider your visitation rights with your daughter."

I was given a fair chance to state my responses. In one of the final stages of the court proceedings, the judge asked me, "I do know you are well read and understand you are familiar with the laws too. Your wife tells me you have recently written a book on American Visa laws. The court will allow you to represent yourself, if you wish to."

My answer came promptly, I said "Your honor, that we are standing here is proof enough that the fate of my family depends on outside help. I may have failed to give her the confidence despite the twelve years of our marriage. But I am confident that if these have not been convincing enough, nothing else will. I'd rather stand here in silence, and listen to her allegations and give her a quiet hear. Today however, I respect her feelings and I am willing to let her go if that is what she wants so earnestly"

After a nod and a brief silence, the judge turned back to my wife, and asked her this last question - "I have heard from both the sides. I want to ask you one last time before it goes on record - Will you go back to your husband and be a family again? On the next assigned court date, I will announce my judgment"

Her answer came immediately, as if she had planned on being asked.

I guessed, she knew already that the due diligence had been done with her family's help and the judge only wanted to know it as a formality. "Where do I go, your honor? Why should I go to him when he himself is staying in an ashram? He has no house, no savings, and no medical insurance. His health is falling, as you can see. What will happen to me and my child if he dies? "– my wife asked the judge.

How do I confront her? How do I communicate my grief to her when her eyes choose to see what they wanted to see? How do I tell my dearest that she was not wrong? I had failed as a provider, but not because I chose to. American companies owed us money, but they were protected by the country's laws. We were victims of abuse. We were nonexistent, and were cast aside when we did not have anything of value left to offer. It was only us that mattered, and we had to stick together, at times such as these.

But now, all that mattered, all that I wanted to do was to see her, even if it meant to see her less, every time she was in the courts. And as I got to see less of her as the case progressed, giving her the benefit of knowing she was right - Right about her wanting to make her own decisions independently and be in control of her own life, that she couldn't do the twelve years we lived in The Americas. Right about making the decision to live life separated from us. Right about wanting her freedom back.

I was content knowing her health was getting better and that she had been taking care of herself. She had a changed hairstyle, wore new clothes and looked much better. I was glad; she had been accepted back in her own family. I was content knowing my child will have a safe future, even if it was known to me that it would be the last I would see my child. Our marriage was annulled and we were no longer husband and wife. The divorce decree was granted, with no maintenance and no visitation rights to my daughter. Today, after twelve years, the fight seeking visitation rights towards my daughter has taken its slow death.

Our divorce in 2002 was swift. It took less than a year to get the divorce; I did not contest her allegations. The allegations based on cruelty were that I could not be 'settled' in a job. That I have a tendency to switch employers and hence do not have the stability to hold on to a job, further more I was accused of prohibiting my wife from working and my suspicious nature was blamed for it. Allegations, that were extremely difficult to prove, especially at a time when the "dual employment" that was unique to guest workers or "dependant spouses on H-4 visas not allowed to work" were unknown in India.

I did not contest her allegations; neither did I hire a lawyer because I had given up on life altogether. Recovering emotionally as well as from the physical illness, I was in a state of shock and felt betrayed by allegations from all sides. Having lived together and knowing the challenges that we went through together as a family, I had hoped she'd stand by me as she always did in the past, instead I was in a deeper shock with her reverted stance, with accusations that were incorrect. Her lawyer had threatened me with pressing the 498(A) charge of the Indian Penal Code. Under the 498(A), parents of the accused spouse would be picked up and put behind bars irrespective of their location in the country. It did not matter, that me and my wife had arrived into India just a few months ago, and have been living in a foreign country for more than ten years at a stretch. My parents, both aged 70 plus, were shifting residences from one family to another due to this fright. I did not wish to drag them in the muck of allegations that I had indirectly subjected them to.

Her lawyer too, was just doing his job and he found in me a gullible nonresident Indian, who was penniless and broke. I made it a point to feed information on the issues of dependant spouse visas to his inbox over the years post our divorce. I even made introductions with him and the subject matter experts on immigration, especially while he was visiting Canada and the United States!

A foreigner in my own country, with no money, no support system, and very low threshold to sustain emotional agony, I chose silence to be the best option available. However, I made it a point to be present for each and every hearing. As the proceedings were underway, I hoped for her to read between the lines and to understand me, and know what had really transpired, and of what I was going through. I thought of sharing with her things that I had not shared when she was herself under the weather, and when there were threats to our lives. I blamed the guest worker visa laws, that allowed foreign workers to be abused and humiliated--their rights violated. I so wanted her to stay with me through these troubled times, as she had in the past. I did not contest, because inadvertently in a court of law, there was no win: win. One side had to lose. I did not want that to happen. Both sides were my family. Silence was the best option available then. And so I remained true to her allegations - "guilty as charged".

As her lawyer claimed my 'mental imbalance' by virtue of me being declared insane; I was left to my own self, cast aside as a worthless decayed vegetable, waiting for life to unfold the truth. Truth that would allow me the time to prove that I was nothing but a victim of the laws of the country that allowed individuals to be abused. As I recovered from my illness, I have traveled back to the United States and had been employed heading the IT department of a large television channel, hoping the allegations of being irresponsible and professionally unstable were proved untrue. I hoped one day the truth will come out, and I would once again be proved 'not guilty as charged' and allowed to reunite with me daughter.

However, throughout the entire time I was back in India back then, I did observe that despite the highly paid and highly educated working class of the Information technology companies, their families had no idea whatsoever of the H1-B work visa program. To make it even more difficult, I also observed that those involved in the Indian judiciary, including the lawyers, had no knowledge whatsoever of the growing matrimonial discord especially amongst those Indian nationals living life in penury while overseas on work visas. Empathetically, the core issues that lead to the "irrevocable breakdown of marriage" was completely ignored. Corruption sat on the helm of the subject matter, instead of taking a holistic approach to the cultural issues of conflict.

I gradually became aware of the possibilities of creating space for Indian knowledge workers that were on the guest worker visas in the United States. I had come to the United States to take part in the American dream, to build a new life for my family. What I didn't realize was that H1-B visa rules—and more specifically the organizations that learned to abuse them—would make it impossible to realize that dream. I realized that I was not alone. There were many others who struggled with similar challenges, who were exploited in similar ways. I realized that I had the opportunity to shine a light on the exploitation directed at foreign workers, to raise awareness both in India as well as the United States about the challenges faced by those already present and those contemplating a move to the United States. I wanted to be able to change the way the system looked at foreign workers and hoped to bring respect and dignity to them.

Having lived through my own life in the US, I saw this as an opportunity for me to be heard. I hoped to communicate with my wife and our respective families through my work. As Indian workers that were indentured and serving involuntarily with their scheming American employers, they imparted unhappiness which made injustice invisible, hurting families and destroying the core of human values. This 'fight for right against the might' made sense and was worth its weight for the higher cause of fighting for the rights of those affected workers. The renewed enthusiasm and the possibilities were endless. The daunting challenge of reaching out to many was achievable by simply getting online. Being a software developer and on an H1-B visa was indeed a blessing.

I had sought redemption and this was the best way to start. Rather than saying, I found my destiny… destiny had indeed found me!

I began the National Organization for Software and Technology Professionals, (NOSTOPS), in 2004, to be able to change the dominant nature of the guest worker visa programs and making them more employees friendly. Due to the employer centric nature of the guest workers visa programs, a growing number of individual's and their families with valid visas, risked being in status limbo, making them more vulnerable to employer pressure. With negligible whistleblower provisions for the guest workers to report abuse, the work visa programs have been used to prevent workers from organizing and defending their workplace rights.

The National Organization for Software and Technology Professionals, (NOSTOPS), was formed to be able to change the perception of foreign workers earnestly sought by local employers.

To make this possible, generating awareness to the plight of workers and to communicate the common issues that divide and segregate local as well as foreign guest workers was important. And as a first step, representation of these indentured guest workers was a greater need. It was necessary to build a platform for individuals to connect and come together to address issues and to seek help.

NOSTOPS.ORG has emerged out of a personal blog that I used as a platform to vent my personal hurt, and the journey has brought together individuals in similar challenging situations with a single aim of being a common voice advocating the need for change. It has emerged out of a simple need – To fight to change things, and not fight to punish. Not fight to teach a lesson rather fight to be heard and to be a collective voice to bring about the change that affected many.

Over the years, NOSTOPS has over a million subscribers and has participated in identifying the grey areas of labor recruitment as a result of the numerous feedbacks from members via the media campaigns we lead. On numerous occasions, the content that was available on NOSTOPS and written exclusive to specific causes of human trafficking and the related migration issues has been repeatedly cited by the US Department of Homeland Security as well as the United Kingdom Border Agency. The United Kingdom Border Agency published 'Country of Origin Information Report for India' – and has even cited my work as a reference material regarding 'Forged and Fraudulently Obtained Official Documents'. (12th May 2009 and in January 4th 2010).

To make issues known, I have also been a whistleblower receiving numerous threats to life, including physical assault that required hospitalization. I have recommended issues of hurt that are specific to foreign workers in 'dual employment' and I have traveled to meet in person, policymakers and stake holders of the foreign guest worker visa programs – those that have the power to make the formal change, both in India as well as the United States.

Over the decade that I have spent working full time on the cause of fighting for the rights of the workers, I have seen a common thread, of people desirous of change, of people open to see what lies beyond the effects of a globalized society, and so in part NOSTOPS along with its American tech advocacy partners, and the collective growing member base began working towards a BRIGHT FUTURE of JOBS.

5 CARROT OF A GREEN CARD

Emotionally beaten and bruised, I wanted to know if the events that had occurred in my life in the recent past were specific to me alone and were they coincidental and indeed have a deeper meaning. I sought answers and so I began reading about immigration laws and saw a common thread to what had happened historically.

In my search for meaning I began to become confused—was I Indian or American? With which country did I most identify with? The country that gave me birth and shaped my ideals or the country that gave wings to those ideals, values and beliefs I had learnt in my country of birth?

I think, my life's paradox had to do with America taking away my capacity to earn, while on the other hand, India taking away my capability to learn, as a father. I cannot measure which has a greater impact in my life, a decade of lack luster living, followed by the 6 months of hitting ground zero financially, or the 6 months of trying to survive the families at loggerheads and losing my most precious time with my daughter while trying to emerge out of the muck of allegations from the person I had felt closest to.

Looking back at the years gone by, I also admit, I have not had the courage to stand up and say NO to abuse when I had the opportunity to do so. I did not stand firm with the abuse that was meted out to me by my visa sponsor, repeatedly! I chose to be victimized and simply moved on, hoping the next employer could be less abusive. I was too afraid my visa could be revoked and I was afraid to jeopardize my family's security.

I do acknowledge that over the years, I have given up my fight in seeking my right to visit my daughter only because I was exhausted fighting the corruption in the Indian courts of law – that allowed the separation with my daughter. Ignoring my daughter's needs completely thereby violating her fundamental right to be loved by both the parents in the process.

Today quoting Mahatma Gandhi's words – "Abuse cannot exist without the consent of the victim", is fairly easy, but back then, I was naïve and ignorant. I didn't know much about the existence of labor laws that protected the interests of guest workers like me, working in the United States; neither did I make any effort to find out.

I was in need myself but when I sought, just a number to call, a simple helpline, with a person to speak with, simply did not exist. There were many nongovernmental organizations as well as not-for-profit organizations, but none existed to support foreign guest workers on American soil. Foreign workers that were products of labor and were being treated as a commodity but did not even have a helpline for support.

A call made to the US Department of Labor too came back as a rude shock. I was informed that the Department of Labor was unable to look into the matter of a single individual. I was advised, I should seek the help of a professional attorney instead. Discouragingly, I continued to be bullied and battled with self. Little did I realize then, I inadvertently also continued to victimize my family further.

I began to read about immigration history, in an attempt to understand what had happened to me—to discover whether my struggles were unique, and caused by a personal flaw, or were they more universal. I was an honest immigrant coming to the United States to take part in the American dream—which I tried to do honestly, through the legal system, only to crash and burn, dragging my family down with me. Did I fail the system, or did the system fail me? Were there others like me?

As I began to read, I soon realized that the origins of my own struggles as a guest-worker in the United States pre-date my own birth. Many Indians had come to the United States before me—long before the Information Technology boom.

The first Indians began arriving in the 1940s and by the year 1942, The United States of America witnessed an acute shortage of local workers that were required to work, as laborers, on the expanding railway network in the Wild West. Mexicans from across the border were recruited in large numbers. Many strong and well built Indians from the Sikh community were also hired as they already had the experience of building the railway network in United Kingdom as well as in India under the British rule.

Back then, the process of recruiting workers overseas was pretty plain and simple. Workers interested in working in The Americas had to produce recommendation letters that served as a character certificate validating them as good and efficient workers. A testimonial document or the recommendation letter was a necessary document to get a permit to enter the United States, something which could be easily procured via a bribe. As we gradually move forward in the discussion on the nature and types of fraud in immigration, it would be important to observe that the underling process of procuring similar additional documents over the years has historically created avenues for continued corruption.

The Bracero Program was the United States first guest worker program, which was primarily used to recruit daily wage laborers. Upon their arrival, the workers were quarantined before being parceled out onto the farmlands to do the agriculture work- work for which there was no local talent available.

Yes, Quarantined! Kept away in make shift barracks, secluded and prevented from mingling with the local population until assured that they carried no communicable diseases.

Surprisingly, during the 22 years that the visa program was active - from 1942 until 1964, approximately 4.5 million Mexican laborers alone entered and worked in the United States of Americas. There were elaborate contracts between them and their contractors - that hired them, covering wide-ranging agreements regarding housing, wages, and labor conditions. The contracts also included the withholding of ten percent of workers' wages, which were supposed to go to the government of Mexico. The money withheld was to be given back to workers when they returned home, as a token of appreciation. In reality, this was never returned. Even though there were laws that prohibited abuse of the foreign workers, there were wide spread abuses and poor enforcement of laws.

The recent H1-B visa guest worker program that began in 1990 has a striking resemblance with that of the Bracero Program. Domestic talent shortage of highly skilled workers was the reason why the guest worker program was restarted in 1990. Unfortunately, like most guest worker programs, the present system too encouraged a varied mix of abuses that present day guest workers endured, creating a biased work culture resulting in a growing indentured workforce. Under this work visa program, the visa sponsors too could manipulate the wages and earnings of their sponsored workers. Here too, the guest workers are continued to be cheated of the pay they were promised. Surprisingly employers and contractors were allowed to import foreign workers; even those employers who have had previously violated the labor laws, such as such those that have routinely violated requirements of payment of wages towards working overtime, withholding of workers salary, paying the legally allowed minimum wage, paying for the foreign workers travel and housing, etc.

But what was strikingly similar with the Bracero Program, is that the contributions of foreign workers to social security made were withheld by the government, the benefits of which never go to the foreigner workers or to their country – which is governed under the totalization agreement.

The H1-B visa program was the country's second guest worker programme. The program was started in 1990 as a means of filling a skill shortage of critically skilled workers that could not easily be found in the United States. The programme identified 108 occupations, such as Architects, Teachers, Venture Capitalists, Physicians, Programmers, Systems Analysts, Puppeteers, Religious Workers, Accountants, Business Managers, Journalist,, Actors, Asian Market Researchers, Corporate Attorneys, Chefs, and 93 others that were difficult to source in the United States, and recruited temporary workers to fill that skill gap from overseas.

Initially, temporary staffing originally began with the intent of filling, hard to find human resource from overseas. Talent that was not available locally. The required talent for which work was temporary, the sourcing was done through temporary staffing. And because the agency that brought in the needed talent, the temporary staffing agencies basically performed the role of a head hunter. A per hire fee or commonly known as a finder's fee was all they earned.

Temporary staffing therefore can be vaguely termed as a 'tripartite arrangement' involving client (the company where employees work), temp staffing company (the agency which sponsors visas and links employees and client), and the foreign worker employees. Client pays the cost of employees and a service fee to the temporary staffing company, with which employees are paid after commissions.

But as these temp staffing agencies were allowed to file work visa petitions on behalf of the companies that needed them, has further paved way for the "per hour salary brokerage" of foreign labor, and similar to the Bracero Program, the H1-B program has become very popular.

Rudely termed as "Body shoppers", they are in fact the temporary staffing firms that filed the work visa petitions for foreign workers to fill the local talent gap, and basically connected two parties – the client companies with the foreign workers, to serve an important function by processing personnel and visa application paperwork.

Large corporations hire talent from time to time as it is a necessary process during their business life cycle. Temporary staffing helps by adding flexibility to their recruitment process. But temporary staffing – the process of sourcing talent from overseas, is painstakingly exhaustive because it is tedious and an elaborate process, Corporations outsource this task domestically to its vendor staffing agencies, allowing corporations to focus on core business. In the mid 1990's, when the influx of foreign workers began increasing, large American corporations decided to refrain from processing visas directly for foreign skilled workers and allowed their vendor contractors to process them instead.

Temporary staffing filled the need; as the need rests on the basis of human issues and the success of an organization is based on the deliverance of these to attract talent – better pay, less working hours, medical and other benefits for family are every day examples of respect to an individual's contribution to its employer.

Though outsourcing the talent acquisition to local vendors was with a good intend, labor recruitment went unmonitored. And because the enforcement of laws was inadequate to control the growing corruption, unscrupulous individuals and firms used unfair, unethical and even illegal practices to exploit a vulnerable group of people- the migrants, a majority of whom did not know their rights.

Because American staffing firms are allowed to sponsor workers from overseas and out place them locally, earning a commission for every hour worked by their foreign workers, it has spawned multiple layers of such 'brokers' that work on third-party commission. This grey market for 'intellectual capital brokerage' may seem necessary to build 'intellectual property' for their employers and even though workers work under sweatshop like working conditions, are in serious violation of human rights.

Take for instance, the case of dual employment specific only to foreign guest workers. Dual employment – where the work visa is owned by one company and the actual work is performed at another. In such a common workplace scenario in The Americas, the foreign workers are tied to their employers like bonded labor throughout the term of their visas.

Because workers are petitioned for visas with a low salary commitment, there are multiple layers of such brokers between the client company and the company that own work visas of citizens from abroad. While a certain company has a couple of benched employees, there are others that have staffing arrangements with the end client that needs workers. Companies try to bid in selling these benched employees at a low price, and in the process end up pitting the benched employees amongst one another in their effort of finding work. While the end client may benefit by hiring an employee with minimal out of pocket expense, it however, adds more to the layers of such intellectual capital brokerage, with each individual agent earning a commission of every hour worked by the foreign employee in the process.

Therefore the resulting 'take home" salary of the foreign worker is always lower than the suggested prevailing wage and is an attribute of temporary staffing gone unmonitored.

This has created not only an indentured workforce of foreign citizens, but has also created a parallel workforce of workers that do similar work, speak the same language and put equal efforts, but compete against one another. This unhealthy compete creates segregation amongst workers and divides them into separate classes – those with rights against those without!

For an American corporate, to begin using the H1-B work visa program, those that required the services of a skilled worker having certain specific skills, and those which were not available locally, was easy. It did not even have to provide evidence that the local talent was indeed available. The organization simply would source the talent through headhunters. These headhunters, typically immigrants themselves, would then make recommendations based out of professional choices available to them from their native land, and recruit qualified candidates from their home country.

The process then was merit based, there was no internet back then and the headhunters would generally recruit through advertisements in local newspapers. Resumes were received, and selected candidates were called at the pre-defined dates for an in-person interview. Once screened for technical knowledge, they were then setup to talk to the client company manager over the telephone, long-distance from the USA. Once approved by the client company and selected, these skilled workers were then offered a contractual agreement as per the Indian labor laws, often binding them for a certain number of years. Their Labor Conditional Application (LCA) petition however was filed by the end-client. The headhunters then received a fixed one-time referral fee.

For many middle class Indian families, getting an all-expense paid invitation to work for an American firm was dreams come true. Soon, every hard-working middle class family wanted their child to be working in America.

The genuine, hard-working, honest candidates were competing against fake applicants, who were assisted by these brokers of intellectual capital to document and file their petition. Many H1-B dependant employers, that I have known personally; never found the need to engage the services of a competent qualified attorney to file a petition for its worker overseas. Rather they filled the visa petition forms themselves. As a result, the industry soon found genuine, hardworking workers competing for jobs with workers that gained entry via fraud. The influx of the past two decades of skilled workers from overseas has proven that a majority of those who arrived have been unaware of the rules & regulations of being on an H1-B visa. And the numbers of these were huge. Today Indian immigrants form the second largest ethnic group in United States after Mexicans.

Once inside the country, the challenges created by these labor contractors exploit these foreign workers and include issues that range from a breach of their employment agreements, withholding of salaries, manipulation of and discrepancies in pay-stubs, denial of medical benefits and many such other.

Prasad was one such indentured worker, fighting for his rights. He had approached requesting assistance in helping him seek justice. He required judicial help in the U.S and wanted to take his visa sponsor employer to courts. His salary was not paid, neither was he given any medical benefits. He was seeking payment towards his salary, for the money that was rightfully his, but was withheld. He was on the H1-B visa in the United States with 2 dependents - a non-working spouse and a 3 year old son. Months later, Prasad won the judgment against his employer, and received full back wages plus additional penalties duly awarded by the American justice system

Today with well over 4 million workers on the H1 visa, the impact of the workers serving involuntarily and those that are beholden to their employers; and their affect on the American as well as the Indian economy is a growing concern. Things may look different today in the sense that unlike Mexican workers that enter illegally, guest workers under the modern day guest worker program come legally but experience similar exploitation.

They enter legally on temporary visas and then overstay beyond the expiration of their visas, in the hope of getting permanent residence. But not all overstay beyond the expiration of their visas. A majority of guest workers simply fall out of their valid visa status, due to the stringent visa laws, that are employer centric and less benefiting of its guest workers on short term work visas.

The visa policies that gave employers a strong hold were so easily manipulated, that when I had myself been repeatedly shunting from one visa sponsor to another, the visas of my wife and daughter too were to be changed to a dependant visa; however, my employer did not do the necessary paperwork that would allow my dependants to be in legal visa status too. And because of the continued visa shunting, I had jeopardized my wife and my daughters visa status altogether.

Because the visa sponsor employer can terminate a guest worker employee at will, simply by issuing a termination letter, it forces the guest workers to be in a precarious visa status limbo situation. Those gaining entry through fraudulent and deceptive means, via manipulating immigration documents, are often stranded when the only means of visa procurement was meant to gain entry into the United States. Alternatively, because the visa sponsors preferred fresh-off-the-boat workers, as they are willing to work at an even low salary, the labor cost differential, creates unemployment for those already present in the country. Employer sanctions therefore create a caste system, amongst workers, where one foreign worker is pitted against the other, but it is the employers that stand to profit.

Once the workers lose their immigration status, they are prohibited to be employed by any business. And since these new illegal workers could not be employed "above the table" as part of the program mandate, they were left on their own in a foreign land, open for exploitation. As a growing number of workers begin working for "cash", instead of the stipulated payroll, results in their unemployment and not receiving the benefits that ensured their citizen's interests.

Needlessly, the advantages of hiring illegal workers are many. Workers without proper immigration documents were willing to work for lower wages, without support, health coverage or in many cases did not have any legal means to address abuses by the employers as they feared being deported. These unfortunately, compete with those workers who come in legally.

The hurt is on both sides

But, it wasn't just the workers that were being affected either! For the genuine employer with an urgent need, finding the right talent is always terribly exhaustive. If observed closely, a vast majority of American companies that advertise for local jobs on career sites and LinkedIn groups are those that are in the temp staffing arena where they don't have jobs but attempt to fill their client's jobs. Being a very competitive space, the companies that can submit the most qualified candidates are likely to then receive approval from the client to place one or more of these workers. In essence, the temp staffing agencies need a wider pool of qualified candidates to present to their clients. These temp staffing companies rely heavily on their good reputation among technical professionals to agree to be submitted for a potential contract. They are in the business of attracting foreign workers for a potential sale to their client companies in their country.

While most recruitment for technical jobs is done online, the process of further filtering through a mass of genuine and fake applicants is cumbersome and creates a downtime in filling the open positions. Companies needing talent thus find temporary staffing a dependable solution that could help segregate the good apples from the bad.

"It is important that reforms today should not be aimed at the creation of more rules that come about with the paranoia of protectionism. Instead, a better and intelligent way is to open the doors to allow smart and talented workforces that will not tie the worker to the employer and at the same time discourage employers from making empty promises of getting a Green Card"

Because the work visa laws are laced by the 'doctrine of dual intent', which means that though the work visas for foreigners are non-immigrant in nature, should an employer feel the need to hire the employee permanently, the employer can sponsor a petition seeking a permanent residence on behalf of the employee. Companies have used the 'Carrot of a Green Card' to not only bind their foreign employees, but have used the work visa laws to control movement of its labor force. Though an essential attribute to control job attrition and labor arbitrage, it has inadvertently led to the jobs getting off shored, because companies have used the visa laws mainly for the purpose of labor mobility and transfer of jobs overseas, and not as a means to offer permanent residence to its foreign workers.

Manipulating work visas

Most American organizations use either the H1-B or L-1 visas categories to bring in talent from overseas. The H1-B and L-1 visas being the two well-known work visas categories that offer the least protection to its foreign workers and are preferred by employers. Both the visa categories have been preferred, but they have their basic differences–

(1) An H1-B work visa requires a company to pay a fixed monthly salary to its sponsored worker. While on the L-1 work visa the company need only pay an allowance.

(2) H1-B visas have an annual quota of only 65,000 visas, plus an additional 20,000; reserved for those with a US education and wanting to return back, while the L-1 visas have a 'blanket provision", meaning there is no quota.

Based on these differences, companies have built around three different business models:-

The first is the pure offshore outsourcing business model, in which companies perform most of their work overseas in low-cost countries. The second category includes companies whose primary business model is not offshore outsourcing but they have built up significant offshore outsourcing operations. The third category is companies that do not yet do a lot of offshore outsourcing.

It will be important to understand how these two work visa categories have in fact tied the importing and 'benching' of its foreign workers to that of the outsourcing of jobs overseas; Outsourcing of visas domestically has led to the Outsourcing of local jobs overseas.

It therefore becomes necessary to view at the core of the underlying issues of unemployment due to the indentured nature of these work visa programs.

From the foreign worker view point, a temporary work visa can be an important first step towards getting a permanent residence, but most foreign workers actually never receive the Green Card. Even before the emergence of the off shoring of high-skill jobs, many H1-B visa holders were never petitioned towards permanent residence by their employers. In the late 1990s, it was estimated that only 50% of H1-B visa holders became permanent residents. The numbers are likely to be worse for L-1 visa holders, because it has even fewer labor market protections than the H1-B.

While the H1-B visa category has received the most scrutiny in the press, we should not forget about the L-1 visa program, which has become an alternative for many companies. Over the years, even though the press reports indicated corporations minimizing their use of the H1-B visas and hiring Americans, but what may appear to have been a decrease in the H1-B visa use, has substantially increased the use of L-1 visas. It appears that companies were replacing the use of the H1-B with L-1 visas.

To understand the preference over the L-1 work visa, let us understand the types of L-1 visas available. There are two types of L-1 visas available- L-1A and L-1B.. L-1A visas are intended for executives and managers while L-1B visas are issued for "specialized knowledge" workers, allowing companies to bring in a wide variety of their personnel from overseas operations. The Department of Homeland Security's Office of Inspector General found that *specialized knowledge* "is so broadly defined that they have little choice but to approve almost all petitions".

In February of 2010, The Economic Policy Institute published a briefing paper written by Professor Ron Hira titled "Bridge to Immigration or Cheap Temporary Labor? - The H1-B & L-1 Visa Programs Are a Source of Both" and had some convincing statistics on the use of the work visas. In 2002, India was the source of only 10% of L-1B visas, but by 2005, as offshore outsourcing began to rise, India was the source for 48% of all L-1B visas issued. And by

2004, the number of L-1B visas issued outstripped L-1A visas. Given the rapid increase in offshore outsourcing since 2005, it was quite likely that a sizable share, perhaps even a majority of L-1 visas, were being used to send work previously performed in America to low-cost countries such as India.

Due to the rapidly accelerating globalization, the use of the guest worker programs by American companies have evolved. Quite a few many companies used the guest worker programs as a means for facilitating knowledge transfer—transfer of work and knowledge to its overseas operations in low cost countries. And American companies often do the replacement of domestic work and the foreign workers through their vendor contractors. These same contractors that bring in foreign talent, without having real jobs to go to, and in cases where there was work available, exclude American citizens from even applying for these jobs.

Though the modern day visa program serves the needs of the host nation as well as those that directly benefit via outsourcing of its workers, it has now become imperative to bring our attention to the provocative abuse of the same in order to guard our common interests.

Modern day slavery

The modern day guest worker programs are abused, and the growing incidences of abuse, compels some to still prefer to call it 'modern day slavery'.

Under the modern day guest worker programs, the subjugation of human spirit is evident. The suppression continues to subdue foreign workers because of being tied to their employers restricting their mobility and the freedom to choose their employers. Though the program intent rests on managing the labor flow, the program hurts its own citizen workers as well because they are excluding from the labor market, because companies prefer to hire foreigners with work visas. In the process of our understanding, it will be important to consider how the laws have created two classes of workers – on one hand, the visa laws allows American companies to bond foreign workers via elaborate employment contracts and on the other hand, exclude local American workers from even applying for jobs – jobs that are specifically advertised for foreign workers.

So how does this affect in the overall economic and social well being of the members of the society?

With the abundant and easy availability of foreign workers via H1-B and L-1 visas, coupled with loopholes that allow below-market wages, companies have had little reason to hire American workers. But, why were these firms not interested in hiring American workers? Companies rely on the H1-B and related L-1 programs for three principal reasons.

First, it facilitates their knowledge-transfer operations, where they rotate in foreign workers to learn jobs done by American workers.

Second, the H1-B and L-1 programs provide them an inexpensive, on-site presence that enables them to coordinate their offshore functions. Many functions that are done remotely still require a significant amount of physical presence at the customer site. Guest workers are less expensive than comparable American workers, because the grey market in the brokerage of intellectual capital of foreign workers allows foreign workers to be paid less. A company derives competitive advantages by paying its visa holders below-market wages. This labor arbitrage is a fact of doing work onsite.

And lastly, the H1-B and L-1 programs allow the American operations to serve as a training ground for foreign workers who are then rotated back to their home country to do the work more effectively than they could have without such training in the United States.

According to Professor Ron Hira, "the guest worker program has become bifurcated, with some employers using the H1-B and L-1 visa programs as a bridge to permanent immigration while other employers use it simply for temporary labor mobility. Rather than attracting the "best and brightest" for permanent immigration, the programs have increasingly been used for temporary labor mobility to transfer work overseas and to take advantage of cheaper guest-worker labor."

Furthermore, it has also been observed that most companies do not transfer the work visas of their foreign workers to a Green Card, but in fact 'bank visas'. Companies file visa petitions in large numbers and the keep their excess H1-B workers in their home country and send them to the United States only as the need arises. Companies bank visas of their workers because they themselves do not know what percent of their existing H1-B employees are actively working in the United States. !!!

Surprising enough, the government also does not directly keep a track of the conversion from a temporary to permanent resident status of its foreign workers. Ideally, there could be a possibility to track each individual guest worker and then to identify whether they are sponsored for and later granted a Green Card, but the data available itself is limited. *To begin with, the U.S. Department of Homeland Security (DHS) does not even know how many H1-B or L-1 holders are in the country in the first place.*

The below table shows the total number of H1-B visa holders listed state wise. The data presented is for the year 2007 - The year after the first ever H1-B visa lottery.

	State	Number of H1-B	State Population (2007 estimate)	Number of H1-B per 1000 population
CA	California	184,567	36,553,215	5.05
NY	New York	105,621	19,297,729	5.47
NJ	New Jersey	79,707	8,685,920	9.18
TX	Texas	69,203	23,904,380	2.89
FL	Florida	51,389	18,251,243	2.82
VA	Virginia	48,316	7,712,091	6.26
IL	Illinois	48,267	12,852,548	3.76
MA	Massachusetts	43,221	6,449,755	6.70

PA	Pennsylvania	35,514	12,432,792	2.86
MI	Michigan	30,601	10,071,822	3.04
GA	Georgia	27,572	9,544,750	2.89
MD	Maryland	22,722	5,618,344	4.04
WA	Washington	19,959	6,468,424	3.09
NC	North Carolina	17,149	9,061,032	1.89
OH	Ohio	16,735	11,466,917	1.46
CT	Connecticut	16,392	3,502,309	4.68
CO	Colorado	9,282	4,861,515	1.91
MN	Minnesota	8,625	5,197,621	1.66
MO	Missouri	8,400	5,878,415	1.43
TN	Tennessee	8,370	6,156,719	1.36
WI	Wisconsin	8,072	5,601,640	1.44
AZ	Arizona	7,963	6,338,755	1.26
DC	District of Columbia	7,258	588,292	12.34
IN	Indiana	6,828	6,345,289	1.08
DE	Delaware	5,615	864,764	6.49
KY	Kentucky	5,126	4,241,474	1.21
IA	Iowa	4,912	2,988,046	1.64
KS	Kansas	4,830	2,775,997	1.74

NH	New Hampshire	4,614	1,315,828	3.51
LA	Louisiana	4,468	4,293,204	1.04
OR	Oregon	4,375	3,747,455	1.17
AL	Alabama	4,326	4,627,851	0.93
OK	Oklahoma	4,142	3,617,316	1.15
SC	South Carolina	3,401	4,407,709	0.77
RI	Rhode Island	3,290	1,057,832	3.11
AR	Arkansas	3,190	2,834,797	1.13
NE	Nebraska	2,891	1,774,571	1.63
NV	Nevada	2,831	2,565,382	1.10
UT	Utah	2,490	2,645,330	0.94
HI	Hawaii	2,422	1,283,388	1.89
MS	Mississippi	2,073	2,918,785	0.71
ME	Maine	2,003	1,317,207	1.52
NM	New Mexico	1,917	1,969,915	0.97
ID	Idaho	1,827	1,499,402	1.22
VT	Vermont	1,760	621,254	2.83
PR	Puerto Rico	1,415	3,942,375	0.36
ND	North Dakota	1,068	639,715	1.67
WV	West Virginia	1,049	1,812,035	0.58

SD	South Dakota	898	796,214	1.13
WY	Wyoming	598	522,830	1.14
AK	Alaska	591	683,478	0.86
MT	Montana	454	957,861	0.47
VI	Virgin Islands	230	108,448	2.12
GU	Guam	210	173,456	1.21
FM	Federated States of Micronesia	18	107,862	0.17
MH	Marshall Islands	10	61,963	0.16
AS	American Samoa	7	57,291	0.12

6 PURSUIT OF HAPPYNESS

"Why do bad things happen to good people?" I asked, in one of the daily satsang meetings in the Swaminarayan ashram prayer hall. She had left just two months ago before I had arrived into the ashram from the streets where I was living as a homeless. The ashram prayer hall had about forty devotees, many of whom held regular jobs, arriving for the daily prayers.

The answer, took my back by surprise "Can you tell me how you identify the good and the bad? " – The spiritual guru asked, scanning the room, expecting someone to speak up. After a brief silence, he continued - "You see, Individuals have a tendency to attach themselves with their emotions. This strengthens their identity of who they are. All of us have a tendency to attach our identity of who we are with our emotions. This perpetuates the association of attaching our emotions with the events around us. Emotions by themselves are nothing more than thoughts, and thoughts have no form or body. Events occurring around us are a constant process. So events by themselves are neither good nor bad. It is the human tendency to create an association of events with these emotions. Emotions by themselves are not unhappiness, it is an unhappy story plus an emotion attached to it is what we call unhappiness."

I realized that I had witnessed a series of events leaving me with a lot of emotional pain. Upon my arrival into the ashram, I could connect with the series of events that I had experienced in my recent past. I had witnessed a catastrophic event of 9/11 that justified my emotional pain. Having lived in America for more than twelve years, I had been a victim of abuse due to the color of my skin and have also been a witness of similar events happening with others. I had experienced abuse first hand in the work place by my employers and have also been a witness to a growing trend of visa abuse and human rights violations - happening to others like me. Abandoned after a decade's stay in a foreign country, I had returned back home, and now I was experiencing a divorce. I was experiencing separation not only from the person I cared about the most, but also my only child. And to sum it up, I was undergoing medical treatment for my lung tuberculosis! I felt betrayed!

Having studied and living in the United States for more than a decade, I found myself jobless competing with new arrivals on the H1-B visa. I and thousand other workers with their families witnessed the growing competition and the resulting hatred amongst themselves. And I knew I wasn't alone. Many from India on the guest workers program felt the same. I also knew this was not just limited to the guest workers, American citizens, were hurting as well. They were hurting and they were angry because their jobs were being lost to workers coming in from overseas, who seemingly were willing to get paid a lower salary. Corporations were looking to get more work done at a cheaper cost by sending work overseas. Unfortunately, the experienced guest workers, whose work visas were tied to their body shopper employers, too were replaced by the fresh-off-the-boat workers. I had been the victim of such a practice.

Over the twelve years that I had stayed in the United States, I realized that American corporations depended heavily on foreign labor in order to be competitive and be profitable. But, it was slowly becoming evident; that America was losing its status quo, by treating its workers as a commodity- by making employment at will, while at the same time, bonding foreign workers to the firms that sponsored their visas and making it easier for employers to bypass local talent.

India on the other hand seemed content. The filling of the skills shortages in overseas destinations helped the inward remittances and created employment opportunities domestically, leading to an exodus of outward migration. Workers from India were treated like products that could be sold to corporations overseas, without offering any protection to its own workers. They were going overseas, but sending money back. And Indian companies that helped workers find jobs overseas were offered greater subsidies by the Indian government as a reward.

The law of the land requires that workers get a job in the United States before they can obtain a work visa. In fact many Indians did not know this law. Nor was it in the interest of the Indian government to educate them: the growing demand for India's foreign workers in the United States was good for India. It created jobs overseas for potential workers, who sent remittances home. It also facilitated a new industry of businesses in India- Body shopping; that help fill the talent needs on behalf of their American counter parts.

In 2005-06, India had a labor force of roughly 496.4 million people. A sizeable 45%; out of the total Indian population of 1.09 billion were counted as its labor force. And an estimated 14 million individuals entered into the Indian labor force every year. With so many job-seekers, job creation was a top priority.

In mid 2008, while the employment growth rate was estimated to be around 2.7 percent, the population growth rate was 1.7 percent. Ideally this should have been a good sign, but even though the employment growth was more than the population growth, there was still a backlog of those unemployed and those that were unemployable. The growth of employment therefore was not sufficient enough to absorb the new entrants as well as the existing unemployed and unemployable labor force.

Body shopping, therefore was an encouraging solution to push India's knowledge workers overseas, and the remittances creating employment internally for the workers in the informal sector. When Indians moved overseas for work opportunities, both countries stood to gain. In order to make the labor market more competitive, increasing the wages was a need to artificially create job attrition. And job attrition created newer opportunities due to the displacement of labor it thus causes.

Unfortunately, the increased job attrition paved way to employment labor contracts, binding the employees further. The flexibility in the labor market was thus eroded and created multiple layers of

Intellectual Capital brokers, directly resulting in the lowering of wages and large scale unemployment. The reduction of wages as a result of the increased grey market in labor recruitment created a cyclic phenomenon of worker abuse and human rights violations.

Employers even began sharing amongst themselves an employee databank listing 'black listed employees' - employees that showed a tendency to 'jump ship' into an American corporate directly, those that sought freedom from their existing labor contracts. This closed system therefore was put in place to control the movement of its employees, and to induce employee circulation required to balance attrition costs and manage profits.

However, as the world economies shift, with a focus on creating employment opportunities back home, the exodus of the returning unemployed overseas or those caught up in the illegality of the immigration wrangle – of being in 'status limbo', or being 'visa orphans', is an alarming figure and a concern. Many returnees either compete with their domestic workers or end up becoming entrepreneurs maintaining ties with their American counterparts leading to more local jobs outsourced. The economic inter dependencies between workers from both the nations is hence indispensable.

As people movement was reduced to the function of greed, to me, it seemed that the increasing digital divide had created two separate classes of workers – those with workplace rights and those without. I realized that in order to avoid abuses liked the ones I suffered, I needed to first raise awareness and plug the immigration loopholes that perpetuated fraud; and that mandated a deeper understanding of people movement and human migration across borders. The good intent of hiring the best and the brightest was being lost, and the visa program was severely abused. America's dependency on foreign labor without adequate protection of rights for their own workers or for those coming in as invited guests was creating a growing pool of subjugated individuals. It was time to not only bridge the digital divide, but on the contrary, build a bridge across the seven seas that separated two great nations in a long lasting partnership.

As workers rights were violated, there was increasing evidence of the incomplete buried emotional pain of individuals that was manifesting into a larger collective emotional pain. Pain that was pitting one class of workers with the other creating a widening gap between the workers- while the American workers blamed foreign workers taking away their jobs, those on guest work visas, sought better pay, better living conditions and an opportunity to be a part of the American dream.

The emotional pain was felt on both the sides, and was increasing. It was required to build awareness to the issues that were common to both the sides. Both the resident as well as foreign born citizens on short term guest worker visas, including those that were looking to make America their new home therefore had to come together as a collective workforce in defending a common identity - one that would collectively bring a reform to the immigration and labor recruitment policies, because the work visa misuse was not limited to Indian companies alone, but the American owned firms as well.

Both sides sought independence and freedom from being victims of greed, but we were fighting for our rights individually. Both sides sought independence from the subjugation they involuntarily were subject to. Both the sides were venting out their anger in isolation. But in order to seek independence, both sides had to be worthy of what they were saying, and the worthiness could only come when both the sides were united.

I remember, when I began, I first had to negotiate with fear. I say fear, because at this time the xenophobia was at its peak. America had experienced an attack on their pride. Add to it, the increasing job losses. Most of which were lost to foreigners on short term visas – a majority of those from India. Guest workers, were often blamed for working at lower wages, and hence preferred by the companies, and so blamed for the resulting pink slips. American citizens blamed foreign workers taking away their jobs, largely due to the fact that "dual employment" was specific only to the H1-B visa, was largely unknown... even by the American colleagues sitting in cubicles next to a foreign guest worker. Hate emails were the most common and continued for almost a year, despite having left America.

When I began the dialogue to communicate issues that were specific to foreign workers, hate emails from American workers was a constant activity. It was an enduring process to communicate that both American as well as foreign guest workers were in fact two sides of the same coin. It was the immigration policies that segregated and divided the workforces, Occasional rude text messages or at times threatening phone calls continued.

I decided that I needed to take action – a decision that was not without personal consequences. I put online a database of companies the sponsored visas, companies that needed reviews by the workers themselves. It was a simple people helping people initiative. Any employment offer made by a company, or anyone working for a company that was being abused, could receive feedback from other workers on a public forum. The idea was to bring transparency, build awareness and also encourage individual workers to speak against fraud and abuse by their employers. Individuals that acted as agents in India for their American employers, those who had the role of finding the local talent to outplace them in the United States, found my efforts a threat. As a result, over the years, I have been threatened, physically assaulted repeatedly. And each time this happened, I went into hiding and frequently changed phone numbers.

"Who the hell are you to post a comment on our company? Don't try to be a mahatma. Or you will end up just like him" - I remember these words distinctly, as I received a fist on my left temple on the head.

But as much as I wanted to maintain a low visibility, it was getting imperative due to the volume of reported abuse that a dialogue with the other side - the policy decision makers needed to be established.

It was therefore required to take help from the media and to create an awareness campaign on the issues of foreign workers being subjugated by their employers. The employer centric nature of the visa program was creating an indentured workforce, but now the workers were standing up and speaking for themselves.

Back then, I often felt offended when I read reports in the media on the plight of the foreign workers – I felt like journalists were exploiting the grief of their own workers. I began meeting with journalists, explaining what had happened to me, and what is also happening to others in similar challenging situations, but no one wrote about these problems. Reporters did not seem to understand that plight of foreign Indian workers abroad – and by refusing to report stories of the challenges, like the ones I faced, I felt that the media was creating an illusory image of the life in the west

I was your typical techie that knew his technology well but lacked the political will to make the right connections, I did not know anyone back in India because of the years spent overseas, and I was a foreigner in my own country with a thick American accent. The news reports I read online from India, telling me, that the country, where I had spent 12 of my very important years had considered me presumably dead or thought of me as amongst those deported in the aftermath following 9/11. My name was on the memorial wall at the Ground Zero, World Trade Center. The Samar Magazine article, in the United States, that published my name as one of the deceased or deported on 7th of July 2006, asked its readers a simple question – "Are South Asians Missing in the Immigration Fight? "

Back then in India, whenever I made an attempt to best explain the issues regarding the plight of foreign Indian workers abroad that were getting abused by their employers, much similar to what occurs in the gulf, I was ridiculed and scoffed by the journalists. No one believed that an educated Indian could come back from the "land of plenty", as a "failure". With a fragile body frame, due to my illness and the resulting divorce, I had drastically reduced from 86 kilos to a meager 42.8 kilos in just about 5 months. Still recovering from my lung tuberculosis, speaking was a challenge and as breathing got heavier, I often coughed blood. Internet became the best way for me to communicate. I needed to be heard and to tell my story; wanting people to understand and believe me. I knew it would be a long journey – but it was one that I needed to begin.

It started with a web site, which I built from various cyber cafes around the place I lived in Nerul, Navi Mumbai. On the web site were case studies of guest workers, caught in the legal visa issues and the abuses by virtue of being bound via contractual agreements to their employers. Content specific to visa fraud and types of visa fraud, the do's and don'ts of body shopping in the form of frequently asked questions brought back the feedback from the concerned individuals victimized by their firms that were abusing the guest worker program mandate. Building awareness was the key. I even wrote a book "American Work Permit – Official Rules and Regulations of the H1-B program" that offered with explanation the rules and regulations and the translation of 'what the law says"!

I had met (Late) Dr Arun Vakil, Chairman of the Indo-American Society – Programmes, a celebrated author of "Gateway to America", to seek his help. He was very well known and a celebrity himself. I spent a considerable amount of time with him, to explain to him the issues that hurt both classes of workers. He was a great mentor.

His participation helped get the required attention starting a new paradigm in the online world. We finalized content partnership with Rediff, a leading portal for Indians, which helped me to reach out to the prospective millions who sought knowledge on migrating to the United States. I included articles and frequently asked questions such as - Want a job overseas? Beware of fraud, US student visa: When to apply, When to apply for US Visas: NOW, Want to settle in the US?, To be on H1-B or not to be, H1-B visas: 'If rejected, you cannot appeal', etc. The internet had opened a new arena. It helped me to connect with the like-minded and it helped me to reach out to those across borders as well. Because knowledge workers were available online, it was easier to connect with then. I also received a lot of feedback from those that sought an entry into the Americas, as well as those that found the threat of the incoming exodus of new overseas migrants.

To reform the policies that allowed the import of foreign talent on the guest worker visas such as the H1-B, L-1A, L-1B as well as the B-1 visas, it was an attempt to advocate reforms that focused on the human rights violations and workplace abuses. Policy recommendations to overhaul the guest worker visa programs that ensured foreign workers would not be exploited and American workers would not be undercut was central to the theme of my fight for the right. It had affected me. It had affected my family. I had found my calling – and I quickly learned that I was not alone.

As I progressed on the mission mandate of 'facilitating the issues of individuals on the guest worker visas', - which facilitated queries made by individuals stranded, abused and hurt by their employers contractual agreements, the feedback from the workers on guest worker visas grew more intense. There were also many who wanted to meet me in person. Some wanted to discuss the possibilities of 'pushing' talent overseas, while some to threaten against my growing whistleblower activities. To the employees, I was a medium to vent their angst against their employers. Academics also began to talk to me and incorporate my knowledge in to their research.

Some even made ridiculous financial offers which to my bewilderment stood in the correctness of the law, but aimed at illegal activities, such as human trafficking. For instance - Recently divorced, yet with a valid US visa, I was often approached by touts with fabulous offers – to the tune of 1.2 to 1.5 million rupees, just to facilitate and to help unite a destitute spouse stranded in India with her husband - someone who had made a single entry to the United States years ago. The longer the separated couple, greater the amount offered!. A fake marriage in India and then an ex-partae divorce on my return alone was all it took! I was getting introduced to the underground world of human trafficking.

With an average of 300 emails a day, the feedback was overwhelming and also a little scary. But for now, I was glad, I had the attention. It was a difficult time and I did not know whom to trust. I simply jotted down a few alarming pointers, which I referred to as I found a convergence with the migrant worker related immigration issues in the years to come.

During those difficult times when I was a foreigner in my own country, books were my closest friends. Living alone, when I knew only a few friends, I read voraciously. My mind eager to grasp every line of information fed into it. With each book, I found myself identifying with the author. Reading was inspirational. It nurtured my soul, and fed the required spiritual dosage of staying in course on my path in the Pursuit of HappYness.

Looking back today, I realize that over the years, I have connected with some remarkable people, and some extraordinary thinkers, including those that worked in think tanks of the respective countries, and it gave my life's purpose a new dimension altogether. India did not have the ministries setup for the non resident Indians then; neither did we have the social networking web sites.

I remember, it was February 28th, 2005, at 2:30 pm, the last day in the family courts, the day when my divorce judgment was to be declared. I had never missed the court dates, and this was the last day I'd see my wife. The eleven months of court appearances, and today I was to see her leave forever. It was too painful. So instead of opting to be in the courtroom, I opted to not be present,. Instead at the exact date and time that the presiding judge was to be announcing the formal end of my marriage, I was in New Delhi, sitting with a gentleman that I believed would be able to make a difference to my cause. I hoped to communicate with him the need for guest worker representation. I sought his guidance, hoping it could make a difference by virtue of his participation in the existing Indo-US affairs, which included his leadership with the newly established 'United States India Political Action Committee' (USINPAC). Amongst the many hats he wears, Robinder Sachdev also leads the famed think tank - The Image India Institute.

The same day my meeting was scheduled, I had my first media interview appeared in the Computer World magazine in Washington DC. It featured the issue on how the work visa petitioning employers manipulated the Prevailing Wage Rate and other related discrepancies. The article "H1-B Special Report" was the first of its kind, that introduced me to the readers. The article and a copy of a book - "Dude, did I steal your job?", written by an Indian worker on the H1-B visa from New Jersey, was left behind with Robinder introducing him to the world of Indian indentured workers working in the United States. The book was a response by the author to the allegations from most American citizens about foreign workers stealing their jobs in the United States. The book was aptly named – "Dude, did I steal your job?". I left New Delhi, happy and content knowing action would soon begin.

Amongst the many feedback received, I have had some interesting responses from American workers as well. Donna Conroy was the first from the 'other side' that I connected with virtually. She was one of the countless American citizens who had lost their jobs to foreign guest workers. Someone that I stayed connected to date, not only because we had a common hurt, but simply because she seemed to understand the issues far better than anyone else. But there is also a fondness to her. For she was that someone special, who had for the first time since my leaving The Americas had connected and inquired about my life, about the way the change affected my life. She offered to help me seek justice against the body shops and urged me to look at how foreigners on guest worker visas as well as American citizens were in fact two sides of the same coin! My entire journey, today, could not have been possible without her partnership. In one of our telephonic conversations, I remember her words– "My word is my bond. You can trust me."

During our initial dialogues, the concept of In-Sourcing Talent and Out-Sourcing of Visas was addressed in a larger scheme of things – as an issue between people of two countries.

In-sourcing talent was the practice, when the concept of dual employment was largely unknown in either of the countries.

The concept of dual employment that was specific to foreign workers (a majority from India), wherein foreign talent, were sponsored a work visa by one company and sub contracted or outsourced to another company once within the United States. In dual employment, the employee has two active employment relationships. Such a relationship can be onerous as it requires maintaining two employment complexities. In larger organizations, employers often use an intermediary entity to which the employee is transferred and subsequently assigned to a third company.. This model helps avoid the issues related to permanent establishments. And this was the key component of conflict in the space of labor recruitment.

The Outsourcing of Visas usually referred to as employers recruiting workers in one country and selling their labor in another. Workers recruited in foreign countries had to agree to terms as laid forth by their work visa sponsoring employers, thus creating a bonded workforce at the point of origin. The outsourcing of visas, being the focal point in the political debate not only creates workers as a labor commodity , it in fact compels workers to be shunting from one employer to another. As a result, these contingent workers have a short lived work history that soon lose the competitive edge, turning them into a classified 'visa orphan' status, with expired visas and are vulnerable for continued exploitation and abuse.

A work visa to any country is a function of a job, but receiving a salary still remained the condition for a job. While the shipping of jobs overseas is a concern by most in the United States, it is directly linked to issuance of visas for its workers and their existing policies. As demand gets curtailed by legislative policies, elimination of fraudulent practice take center stage in the efforts of bridging the digital divide and unifying the workforces.

Interacting and understanding these points of view, and after a series of emails, and phone conversations between Navi Mumbai and Chicago – myself and Donna and also with others that we interacted with, it was clear that the employer sanctions of the existing H1-B program had indeed created a biased work force – that allowed employers to selectively segregate workers, resulting in a growing digital divide, creating two sub-classes of workers - who do similar work and speak the same language.

The original intent of the guest worker program, of importing foreign talent, when there is a shortage, had long been eroded. The visa program laws were indirectly pitting one worker against the other. When one side of the coin was tainted, the other shone brightly, putting the society at large in a conundrum – affecting many from San Jose in California to San Pada in Navi Mumbai.

The intent of seeking justice for foreign workers rested on the short comings of the American visa policies that disallowed Americans the right to a job first. It was easier to understand now, that when American citizens themselves lacked workplace rights, in spite being in a single employment, how could foreign citizens on guest worker visas those in dual employment seek justice in a country, where the rule of the land is inadequate to protect its own citizens.

In one newsletters sent out by Donna, she quoted one of me from the recent email that I wrote her, I had written angrily – "damn it, it's your own country. If you cannot get the justice, how do foreigners working on American soil, will ever be able to seek assistance". And I really was glad it went out to her list, because soon after, a lot of

American workers wrote back with their support!

In the 4 months of our communication, we shared a lot in common. Donna set up her organization, Bright Future Jobs, that represented American workers, while I having had the benefit of being the on the H1-B work visa and having had gotten off the hamster wheel long ago, had made a willful choice of returning back to begin an organization representing Indian guest workers.

Both our organizations, NOSTOPS and Bright Future Jobs had a common goal – To promote and address Equal Employment Opportunity on behalf of its respective workers. It was to be working nonstop to a bright future of jobs.

The interview on National Public Radio (NPR) – "Crossing East: New Waves, New Storms"; discussed migration from the east and their impact on the American economy. The news segment provided insights of the migration from the East, mainly from China and India. It spoke of the contributions made by Chinese and Indian immigrants – from the "Gold rush" to the present day high tech worker economy. The news feature brought attention to the fact that many immigrants were leaving the country due to human rights violations of many immigrants. I was interviewed as one who was affected and amongst the many that left to their home countries.

The fight for justice pertaining to fraud had many complexities on its stand alone policy framework, adding to it was the rampant corruption and the huge grey market making it even more difficult to contain the loopholes. But, I had the patience and the time to dig deeper. I could have been dead in between the three consecutive ICU hospitalizations of the recent past or could have already committed suicide by now. It was a pursuit, with no deadlines. Partnering with Donna, gave me the power and the freedom to speak and to make known issues that hurt.

As I was interacting with the other side, collecting evidences to prove wide spread existence of visa scams and visa fraud. And as members of the senate, were asked to witness live public chats that served as evidence to the growing visa misuse, a database of 22,000 visa sponsoring companies was put up live and was free for any to apply for a job in USA. While the continued weekly chats on rediff.com invited many to send responses with regards to seeking employment in the USA; it served as live real time evidence for the standing committees on immigration to see for themselves the questions asked in the open forum about seeking work visas for a fee., and the related rampant process signifying acute fraud in immigration. At the time, once again the demand for H1-B visa was at its peak. As a result, in the year 2006, for the first time, a visa lottery was introduced because the supply overshot the demand and petitions for the H1-B visas were to be accepted on a first come basis.

Back in 2004, the anti-H1-B sentiments rested mainly on the fact that foreign workers coming in from third world countries; and the loosely termed 'desperados'; were accused of being ever too willing to work at lower salaries and hence were driving down the wages. The xenophobia had become wide spread, as the foreign guest workers were held responsible and blamed towards the job loss of his/her American colleague. On line discussion boards, openly criticized foreign workers and they retaliated back furiously.

Again, the concept of dual employment that is unique only of the H1-B program was largely unknown then; to the American workers, or to the families of these foreign workers back home. Dual employment allowed the sponsoring company to earn a commission for every hour worked by the sponsored employees. It is a single sided immigration framework, wherein American firms took the help of American lawyers, to seek permission from the American government to hire talent from overseas. The dual employment seemed to add flexibility in recruitment, and was therefore the origin of "labor arbitrage" and was getting to be known in India, where the push of workers was the highest.

Because the work visa was an employment visa, it could not be procured without an employer. An American employer was therefore needed to file a petition on behalf of an alien worker overseas.

As the first visa lottery of the year 2006, justifies the huge demand from India to obtain work in the United States Temporary staffing firms that were engaged in shopping for bodies made money off of potential workers and sold them to American firms. The agencies were also charging aspiring workers huge sums of money in exchange for a letter of employment in a local American company required towards petitioning their work visa. Legally, an American employer petitioning for an alien worker a work visa petition is required to pay the visa fees,. However the visa scamming was so rampant that the agents would charge potential job seekers a heavy fee towards the visa application and the attorney fees as well. This was strictly illegal. Often prospective candidates incurred loan, even sold of their property in India to pursue their American dream. Because there was less of technology involved, like the internet, illegal practices was not known, and so there was no scrutiny or investigations. Even when incidences of such abuse mushroomed, due to the lack of provisions to report abuse, many individuals as well as firms pushed unqualified candidates by manipulating their documents that were required towards filing a work visa petition. Visa scams and visa hustling were at its peak. Getting unqualified people to come and work was hurting existing Indian workers too, because they were first to be replaced by the fresh-off-the-boat workers, those that had little or no work experience and the requisite qualifications.

It therefore became necessary to take a step back, and understand if the impact of fraud was indeed deeper than what it was thought to be. I knew that fraud existed, but now I wanted to communicate and make the quantum of fraud understood to others. A closer look at the factors that perpetuated fraud at source was therefore mandated; because now, there was proof that fraud and abuse existed. I received numerous complaints from our members claiming to have been victims of fraud. Often calling me, upon their arrival in a foreign land to inform me that the company that invited them did not exist! As nationwide investigations revealed existence of law violations. Shell company accounts, unaccounted black money, withholding of worker salaries and several workplace abuses and human rights violations were unearthed.

My new goal was to expose the corrupt practices of body shops to the larger public. The corruption was just not limited to America alone, but across the borders in India as well, where the recruitment and sourcing of foreign workers was rampant. If these visible instances of abuse were growing, one could only imagine the parallel underground economy of the digital world used to source innocent gullible victims. Email addresses that were easily found on job portals were the easiest targets. A false promise of a job in America in exchange for a fee was often used as a bait to lure prospective aspiring workers. With no knowledge of the laws of a foreign land, individuals often falling victims of fraud, found themselves stranded on arrival in a foreign land.

Of all the available non-immigrant visa categories, the H1-B visa is the only Non Immigrant Visa with a dual intent. With no supporting documents required to prove return to the home country after the end of employment. Individuals on other short term visas added further to the annual quota of the H1-B visa pool. The rampant recruitment drives advertised in Indian print media offering cash-for-visa schemes were evident and clearly visible. There was indeed a large scale grey market in India's overseas labor recruitment. My work would begin with my morning cup of tea and the day's newspaper. As I flipped through the advertisements, I took pictures with my cell phone and emailed them across the seven seas to The Americas. Countless such emails finally was good enough reason to speak with the media.

When we spoke to the concerned heads at the television channel in Mumbai; about the rampant abuse, explaining the need to air awareness, the disbelief was evident. Evidence, and an effective knowledge transfer on the rampant fraud in U.S immigration issues and the cash for visa schemes was explained in detail. As a result a sting operation by the television channel was documented in a half hour program on the well known "UNCOVERED" show on the satellite network of CNBC-TV18.It featured a covert sting operation, using a hidden camera exposing the fraudulent practice of agents charging a hefty fee for a US work visa. The show titled "Hyderabad, Bangalore – Hubs of H1-B visa fraud" brought the needed attention. An operation backed by real employment contracts procured by the victims themselves, as well as their testimonies lead to the closure and arrest of many such bogus recruitment agents in many Indian metros. The transcript of the show aired on February 2007 is given below -

"The elusive H1-B visa, for which young software professionals yearn, has been severely compromised. Middlemen are exploiting the system by creating fake IT companies in the United States and obtaining these visas for a hefty sum without even a job.

This leaves thousands of deserving candidates in the lurch since there are only 65,000 such visas issued every year.

For most people, a stamp on the passport is the last hurdle crossed to launch their careers in the US. But for many getting this H1-B visa stamp is just the beginning of a painful journey of exploitation, underpayment, and unemployment.

This is the world of H1-B visa fraud, a well-oiled nexus of fake employers, job counselors and immigration experts. Newspapers and cyberspace are filled with luring advertisements that claim to get you an H1-B for a price tag. So, can they?

Apparently they can. In a busy suburb of Mumbai, one such H1-B consultant is busy carrying out business. We approached them as H1-B aspirants eager to fly to the US. The range of services on offer was shocking. Here is the conversation we had with this agent:

Agent: We will get you a fake employer. He'll file for your H1-B. He will have a proper company and will be a US citizen.

Us: So what happens once we get there?

Agent: The fake employer who files for your H1-B will give you a work permit and will get away and once you get there, this fake employer will give you a no-objection certificate (NOC), saying you can work with any employer.

Us: Will you find me a job there?

Agent: Once you are there, we have people who will help you with contacts. We can only assist you.

Us: How much will it cost?

Agent: $2,250 will be the immigration fee; $2,250 will be lawyer's charges.

Us: Do many people go to the US using this route?

Agent: People who know and who have relatives ask for fake employers. They want to go there on real jobs. . . Because here you won't get a job as good as the one you can get when you are in the

US.

Us: How long it'll take to find a real job?

Agent: Jobs in the US are tremendous. The problem is not getting a job but getting a visa. We will have all the interviews lined up for you and once you get there, you will attend those and find a job.

Using this route, these so-called counselors send professionals to the US practically without a job. The search for jobs begins only after applicants land in the US. Individuals cannot apply for an H1-B visa on their own. Their employer must petition for them. Petitions for this visa begin on April 1 every year.

Once the petitions get approved, the employer sends the approved form to the employee who then appears for the visa interview in his home country. This visa is issued for a particular job but most of the times the so-called visa counselors help candidates bypass this requirement. They take them to the US on fake job letters. But sometimes touts go wrong too and that leaves many holding on to their H1-B visas endlessly waiting to get to the US.

Ramesh was one such victim. This 27-year-old engineer (whose real name has been withheld) narrated his plight from California. He told CNBC-TV18, "I was in India when I found a desi consultant. I got the reference from a friend. This company was basically into IT consulting . . . they took $3,000 from me and told me they'll give me a good job opportunity because they had clients and stuff."

"Till the time I gave them money, they were very courteous and told me that they'll give me a lot of salary and a lot of incentive and bonus. So, I was thinking it was a good company to start with. When my petition got approved and I told them I want to get to the US as soon as possible, their behavior changed. They said we don't have any clients as of now and we don't have much knowledge about your field."

He finally succeeded in getting to the US, although he is still struggling to get his original documents from his counselor.

But everyone doesn't get as lucky as Ramesh. Manoj, an H1-B visa holder is still waiting for the past one year to fly to the US. This 28-year-old was happy working in a leading multinational firm in Hyderabad, till he decided to head to the land of opportunities.

Like thousands of others like him, he too approached a consultant to help him realize his dream to work in the US. His H1-B petition got approved in October 2006 but it was then that his ordeal started. Instead of taking him to the US, his broker took away his visa documents needed for him to take off.

He then asked Manoj to buy an IP phone with a US number and start looking for a job. Manoj spent many sleepless nights talking to his prospective employers in the US, all the time telling them that he was in the US. Most of the time, the job offers fell through when the employers, thinking Manoj was in the US, wanted him to join at a very short notice

US authorities admit H1-B visa frauds are rampant. Last year alone, they found 2,000 H1-B applications suspicious. These applications were returned to the US Department of Homeland Security for reconsideration. The Consular Section Chief, US Consulate, Mumbai, Glen Keiser, says, "We also see people who are going to jobs that we suspect do not exist. These people are unable to describe their projects to us. When we do even a cursory examination, we may find that the company in the US is simply nothing more than just a shell. Neither are they in a position to offer work for themselves nor do they have a client base, where they can send a qualified worker."

This year, 150,000 people applied for the quota of 65,000 H1-B visas. More than 40% of these petitions were made by Indians and the US consulate says a large number of applications that come to them are suspect.

Keiser explains: "We have found to our regret that Hyderabad and Bangalore are centers of H1-B visa fraud and that it is not difficult to walk into an operation and someone rather forthrightly tells you that they can produce anything to appear to qualify for an H1-B visa. And, in fact, we have had our employees conduct such operations and walking into such agents' office and ask questions."

The US consulate in India is increasing manpower in its fraud investigation team. They are also taking a tough stand against such fraudsters. As Keiser says, "We take such cases very seriously. If we can verify that you are presenting a fraudulent case to us, we will bar you for the rest of your life to enter the US. If we find out that you as an agent are assisting someone to illegally enter the US, we can even bar you from getting any kind of US visa."

But while the US government toughens its stands against such fraudsters in India, these consultants continue their business in broad daylight. A few consultants told us that, they can illegally get us smaller jobs in the US, till the time they find work for us that is suited to our qualifications.

One consultant told us, "You can work as a waiter or in a convenience store till you find a job. A lot of people do that. After all, you would have spent so much money in getting the H1-B visa."

Keiser says, "This is not legal. We are not taking in people to pump gas or to bake donuts. This visa is to bring in specialized knowledge workers to the United States and make them work for jobs they are qualified to do. That is to say, if I am a computer programmer, I am going to do computer programming and not pump gas till the time someone finds me a job of a computer programmer."

It's a vicious circle -- scamsters eat up the H1-B quota and force genuine Indian companies to depend on them for their manpower requirement. Valid for six years, H1-B visas allow highly skilled foreign workers to work in the US in specialized fields like IT, computing, accounting and finance.

Last year, out of the top 10 companies that received maximum H1-B visas, 7 were Indian firms.

Pradeep Udhas, global head, sourcing advisory, KPMG, says, "Today, India's software companies are booming. They depend a lot on H1-B visas because their business models are such that they need people to be onsite. Their business models won't work if the H1-B visas are not given."

Last year, nine Indian IT companies bagged about 20,000 of the 65,000 H1-B visas issued. Seven Indian companies including Infosys,

Satyam, Wipro and Tata Consultancy figured in the top 10 receivers of H1-B visas globally. Yet, Wipro got only 24%, while Infosys managed to get only 20% of what they petitioned for. Both the companies petitioned for 20,000 H1-B visas each. Wipro got 4,908, while Infosys got 4,002 H1-B visas.

Immigration lawyer, Poorvi Chothani explains, "We represent a lot of IT companies who petition for their H1-B visas. This year, with a lot of petitions and the lottery system, we fear we will not be able to get them even half of their requirement."

The H1-B visa crunch forces these companies to hire from the H1-B workers' pool of these scamsters. and that too at a premium. Udhas says, "A lot of these IT companies are then forced to talk to these 'onesy-twosy' consultants and say, 'Okay, you give me your people.' These consultants take a huge cut for providing the services of these H1-B workers, without adding any value."

This is why most of the professionals who land up in the US on H1-B visas find a job within a few months with a genuine IT company. However, this is not the end of their misery. In most cases, the employee ends up getting only a part of his salary while the fake employer pockets 25% to 45% of his salary.

But even when dreams shatter and people end up working for jobs that they are over-qualified for, they shy away from reporting their 'fraud employers.' That is because they go away, leaving behind family and friends and expecting good prospects. They are shattered when the reality turns out to be much bleaker than what they had expected. And it is this hope that keeps the cash registers of these scamsters ringing. Also, it is this flame of hope that allows thousands of gullible candidates to continue to be victimized by these visa touts."

7 LOBBYING FOR CHANGE

Even though the demand for the H1-B visa has always been high and has been consistently increasing, there was now enough evidence to prove that foreign workers were subject to tremendous abuse – abused financially in order to enter the United States, and once inside the country - they were underpaid, or their salaries were withheld, they were bound by elaborate employment agreements that disallowed them to change employers, and many other similar abuses.

Be it the outward migration from India or the influx of Indian foreign workers into The Americas, the factors were non complacent to the original intent of the visa program mandate. In either case, it was the employer that stood to benefit the most.

Employers seeking to hire foreign workers had to agree to certain attestations. Certain terms and conditions were laid down for the employers, amongst them was that the employer would prohibit any of its employees from going on a strike or a lock out. Failure to do so, the employer would be penalized by the government.

On the 3rd of June 2006, soon after the first H1-B visa lottery was announced, despite the knowledge of fraud in the recruitment of Indian workers, it became necessary to get the attention to certain issues that hurt the Indian workers. In retrospect, I had called in a 'sick-in strike' – where Indian guest workers in the United States reported sick at work. This was a protest aimed at seeking the attention. The abuse was rampant. There was an urgent need to halt the corporate need for more overseas talent, before the existing loopholes were contained. The article in Financial Express, published from New Delhi was titled "Indian techies in US plan for a sick-in strike". It sought Indian guest workers serving in the United States to say NO to abuse and to take charge of their own plights against their 'broker' employers. The article highlighted the core grey areas that made guest workers vulnerable.

The intent for the sick-in strike was not to contest authority, but was simply a message to the foreign workers, to observe disobedience by reporting sick at work. It was an attempt to seek attention – to be noticed and to be heard by the policymakers on The Hill. The intent was aimed at seeking the attention and the result was fruitful.

I was invited to Chicago and then to the Capital Hill to testify the existence of abuse and the victimization of Indian workers, large scale visa fraud and the related misuse of the work visa programs. Evidence proving visa scams and visa hustling and the loopholes in the system were to be proved. My 2 month trip to the United States had only one purpose – to be vocal about the common hurt, and to aim to bring about change – change that will unite both classes of workers!

I had to get a visa of course! And so after 16 years, since my first US visa interview in 1991, I once again presented myself at the US visa consular window in Mumbai. Equipped with letters of invitation and an extensive itinerary of meetings with policy heads in Capital Hill, along with a detailed agenda of speaking engagements in different cities, I hoped there would be no questions during the visa interview. To my surprise, I was asked – "How am I to be sure, you are not going to The States to mop floors in Mac Donald's?"

Things had indeed changed over the years. The perception of Indian workers seeking visas had been reduced to the fragment of dollar seeking hungry desperados. But then, there was truth in the question - fraudulent visa applicants had increased over the years. Gone were the days of respect and acceptance. Visa interview was therefore a process of being considered a fraudulent applicant until proved otherwise, and the only possibility of getting the privilege called a visa; rested in proving innocent intent.

My reply was quick and blunt. "Why would I need to travel so far to do just that, when the same is available here and now? The real reason for my travel is to testify abuse of the visas, and to offer what I know, to those that want to hear. What you have in front of you is a list of those wanting to hear my story, amongst them a few senators"

I flew the very next day. It was a long flight with brief stopovers from Mumbai to London to New York and finally to the Chicago's O'Hare International airport. It was already winter and it was snowing. As the passengers made way out of the aircraft, the air outside was extremely welcome. The air was fresh and light, so unlike Mumbai's humid, polluted and damp tropical weather.

As I stood in the long line of passengers approaching the immigration kiosk, I found myself to be anxious. As the queue inched forward, I fumbled through my passport wallet time and again, making sure my papers were in order; preparing self to the questions that may be asked. It wasn't the inadequate sleep or the tiredness from a long flight, neither was it the jet lag, I realized the anxiety was in facing a uniformed federal officer. Would there be anything in the centralized immigration system that had me listed and taken in for interrogation? I had been considered to be dead or deported, according to an article I had read online from India. Would I be put in prison again? Would I be subject to more emotional agony? As I neared the end of the queue, I looked at every officer sitting behind their desks one by one. Trying to read them, assessing them from the distance where I was.

At the immigration desk, I was asked the routine - purpose of my visit, the duration of my stay, place of stay. There was a long silence as the officer examined my papers that included the passport with the extra stapled booklets proving my extensive overseas travel over the years, the letters of invitation as well as the speaking engagements. Without looking up from his examination, the officer asked – "What was the purpose of your visit, again??"

"Testify in the US Congress against misuse and abuse of the guest worker H1-B visa program", I replied without hesitation.

My heart stopped beating momentarily, as the officer looked up at me from the desk he was sitting at. As he tried to get up, he asked me – "What makes you sure you will be listened to? ". As he walked past his desk, he beckoned 3 other officers to come by the desk where we were standing. My heart was pounding; as I see other immigration officers approach our kiosk. It must have been the innocent adrenaline burst that brought about the smile over my lips. I must have spent about 20 minutes explaining to them- the issues of visa misuse, the wage discrimination, dual employment, the abuse of foreign workers via contractual bondage, about my organization and the work it does, the purpose of the visit and the attempts to restore less fraud in immigration.

I was no longer anxious; I was in fact speaking with enthusiasm. I was here to speak and what better listeners than the immigration officials at the port of entry, who have turned back many for not possessing proper documents. Who else but them whose job is to identify fraud at the port of entry?

The excitement was evident in my speech and in my body language, as I spoke graphically moving my hands, to best articulate my thoughts. Their affirmative nods only convinced my beliefs further. At the end of the discussion, as each of the officers shook hands with me wishing me luck, one of them said," Mr. Dubhadkaar, if what you say is possible, the next time you arrive, and if I am to ever meet you again, I will personally give you an extension of stay in The Americas. Hope you achieve what you have come here for". Handing me my passport, he then walked a few steps with me, pointing to the nearest exit.

The uniformed federal officers were very polite and spoke to me with great respect, compared to what I had experienced the last time I was in The Americas. Out in the lounge as I stood at the coffee counter, I heard a voice behind me tell the counter person in front of me, "This one's on me." Turning back, I see the same official pointing at me as he walked past. He smiled at me and said - "Welcome to America, Sir"

With a coffee cup in hand, I walked past the revolving doors. Once outside, I slid myself to a side, for a smoke, waiting for my pick up. The fresh cold winter night was refreshing. The recent snow flurries on the ground still had not melted yet. I was overwhelmed and I was speechless. I let tears roll down my cheeks. It was good to be back!

The days that followed were full of enthusiasm and profound excitement. As I toured the cities speaking with individuals, I was aware that the guest workers from India were particularly disliked, by those that did not understand the nature of the immigration laws of their own country that created the divide. Television anchor Lou Dobbs had done a great job of convincing people that Indian sweatshops owned the exclusive rights of being corrupt and that no American firm was involved in driving down the wages. He was the Jerry Lewis of the anti-H1-B hysteria. Loved by many, disliked by many – the gap of worker classes however, was wider than what was imagined to be. On the flip side, I was thankful that since my last visit, the issues now had reached mainstream media. I was positive, a right message and this gap would be just one big force that would collectively address the 'need for change'.

I remember being taunted in a public forum as being as loose cannon and that I went about naked and bare feet advocating rights. To me, I just didn't care. I spoke to anyone that approached and I also spoke to people in a group. And I spoke to a large gathering of people standing behind a podium as well. I was open to anyone that wanted to hear - about how we were two sides, but of the same coin. How the hurt is common and why we needed to come together and collectively ask the government to bring stronger enforcement of its laws that were easily manipulated.

I was also invited to speak to a small group of about 20, at a private dinner. I never knew their names; neither did I know anything of their professions. I was simply asked to be prepared to address these people and speak to them and answer any questions they may have. I was out there to communicate. I was out there to speak of a common language - 20 people or 2 million, I just didn't care.

I was fortunate enough as I realized later, the small group of individuals with whom I spoke with, were in fact heads of national organizations; some representing the minority communities, staff members of the senate, chief editors of leading publications as well as a handful of those with various governmental departments including the Homeland Security, Department of Labor as well as the Department of Justice. I should have known better, but I was too naïve, and still with a techie mindset, but I spoke with eyes wet and an occasional lump in my throat.

I had arrived in Chicago on the 6th of December, 2006, and the holidays were just a few days away. Christmas was round the corner. The holiday spirit was extremely spiritual and healing. Of the many accommodation options available, including the Marriot, I preferred the YMCAs at the City Of Evanston, in Cook Country in Illinois. I was here in Chicago, on a short visit, primarily to speak on the plight of foreign workers with families who earn very low wages; I was out here because I myself had lived in poverty by virtue of being on the work visas. The YMCAs therefore were the best choice.

The YMCA at this time of the year housed many destitute individuals that required a shelter during the severe Chicago winters. The YMCA housed these individuals because they did not have families or anywhere else to go to – this was something that I could relate to very well and so I blended right in.

Conveniently located near the train station and at the center of the business district of the city of Evanston, the YMCA was a hop away from the busy marketplace. The room window opened into a long street strewn with movie theatre, restaurants, malls, and shops on either side.

The holidays had begun. The shops glittered with discount signs. Christmas carols and music filled the streets, as I walked past the shops, I was glad I was once again in The Americas for Christmas after a gap of 5 years. It was a wonderful experience. I missed Sujata and my daughter terribly. I had not heard from them for almost 3 years now. But I was hopeful. I was hopeful of my visit to The States and desperately prayed that my visit could serve the purpose.

The night of 24th December, 2006, in Chicago was cold, with the falling snow outside. The much acclaimed movie, 'Pursuit Of HappYness', was released that evening, and I watched the movie twice in a row – back to back. The movie made a profound impact immediately. It reinforced my own personal journey. It was an evening to remember. In the 3ft X 7ft room on the 7th floor, of the YMCA, while I cried and prayed in solitude, Jack Daniels kept me company through the night!

In about a week's time, I would be in the Capital and meeting with those that could help make the difference. Donna had said, "Rajiv, This is our time. We will be the first to bring their attention. They too will be surprised to hear what we have to say, you'll see. So don't you worry?"

Donna and I would be flying to Washington DC on the 1st of 2007. We would be required to testify with evidence and I would be grilled. I had come prepared. I had printed only about 80 copies of my research which documented details of visa fraud. I was ready and I was armed!

In Washington DC, on Jan 2nd, 2007, on the first working day of the 110th Congress, at 10 am, we began making the rounds in the House of Representatives– walking door to door to each and every Senator's office, relentlessly making presentations, making sure our issues were heard. We literally visited every Senator's office, spoke as per the allocated time, then walked to another office and repeated the same over again. At each visit, leaving behind a copy of my book.

The effort was not unnoticed. We were invited the next day to sit down and explain the problems in depth, and went over every minute detail that explained the loopholes in the program. With us both on one side of the table, there were seven on the other, throwing at us open questions consecutively. Questions that required immediate answers and these needed to be backed by actual numbers. The five hours we spent in the conference room were terribly exhaustive.

For the very first time, grey areas were pointed out. Areas that not only hurt the Indian workers, but those that create a divide and denied the local workers from being able to apply for jobs and to be in a healthy competition alongside the foreign workers were pinpointed.

I showed evidence of document manipulation – how the salary of a foreign worker could be withheld and how the salaries could be manipulated, with real proofs taken from our members before hand.

I proved evidence of rampant fraud in the process of outsourcing of visas and most importantly documentary evidence was submitted proving that the foreign workers were severely underpaid and how the companies could go unnoticed even when they under paid their employees. Further, how the brokerage and per hour commission actually resulted in foreign workers getting underpaid. It was communicated that the employer sanctions within the visa program allowed a sponsoring employer to fire an employee at will by simply issuing a termination letter, labor bondage by virtue of elaborate employment agreements, as part of the pre-hiring process overseas prohibited the foreign workers from the freedom to choose their employers. Foreign workers were beholden to their employers and served involuntarily. There was a need to encourage and offer protection to whistleblowers. How foreign workers present in The Americas, could not stand up against the injustices as there were no whistleblower provisions for those that seek help, was communicated and agreed upon, as the first step towards reinstating the original intent of the work visa program.

When we finally stepped out of the building, it was already 8 pm. The snow outside was much welcomed. Exhausted, but thrilled by the events of the day. Our inputs were to be thought over. And eventually were put together in a new visa proposal that was to be titled the "H1-B and L-1 Visa Fraud and Abuse Prevention Act of 2007". A legislative proposal would be drafted with an aim to reduce fraud and abuse in certain visa programs for aliens working temporarily in the United States.

The reform bill was aimed at keeping both the work forces in mind treating them as one. But most importantly it put into place whistleblower provisions for the guest workers, with an important provision that the reported fraud *must* be investigated by the Department of Labor as and when a foreign worker reports fraud.

It also included that it was the responsibility of the government to print workplace notices that boldly informed foreign workers their rights and a number to call in case of abuse by their employers. Also printed handouts were to be given to new visa applicants during the visa application process in their home country educating them of their rights as guest workers while working in The Americas.

In a nutshell, the first H1-B visa reform bill "The H1-B and L-1 Visa Fraud and Abuse Prevention Act of 2007" that had a bipartisan support was introduced with the following remedies:

- The bill would require that before an employer may submit an H1-B application, the employer must first advertise the job opening for 30 days on the Department of Labor web site along with summaries of all H1-B applications received
- The bill would require that employers can not advertise a job as available only for H1-B visa holders
- The bill would give the Department of Labor the authority to review EMPLOYERS H1-B applications for "clear indicators of fraud or misrepresentation of material fact", besides the existing "completeness and obvious inaccuracies"
- The bill would give authority to the Dept of labor, permitting them to initiate its own investigations and removing the requirement of the Dept of Labor Secretary to personally authorize an investigation
- The bill will merge Dept of Homeland Security and Dept of Labor in sharing information regarding employers not complying with the program requirements
- The bill will strengthen the whistleblower protections for an H1-B worker and establish new provisions for those on the L-1 visa program
- The bill acknowledges and stipulates that it will be the responsibility of the government to provide information to the guest workers informing them about their rights
- The bill prohibits employers employing H1-B visa holders, from withholding the immigration documents of their employees and will produce them upon request by the employee.

It had been three years since I had embarked on a self assigned journey; in the Pursuit of HappYness. It was a great relief acknowledging that I was once again in the United States, a country, which I had exited from out of exasperation. This time, I was invited, I was respected and what I had to say was listened to. Not only that, but what I had to say would actually be used to bring about a change in the system. The visit to the Capital Hill and the support from the policymakers has indeed been a reward.

During my visit, I kept my newsletters active. I blogged of my daily events during my travels, the people met, the arriving reforms, the proposals drafted, as I sent out newsletters to our mailing list. I continued to communicate with the supporters. And the support was overwhelming.

I was in New York City and in my last leg of travel after visiting Washington DC. I had taken a bus ride from Chinatown, in Washington DC to the China town, in New York City. I could not have ended my tour without a visit to what remained of the World Trade Center, the Ground Zero. I wanted to end my tour with a visit to the same place, where I had begun my journey.

With a successful tour, it would have been a dream come true to set up a presence in the United States. I dreamt of a dream, of setting up the organization that could continue to cater to those indentured and beholden to their employers. And it could begin with a simple helpline, which could be the available to the guest workers. The feedback and the issues of workers could continue to be communicated with the policymakers at Washington DC. It was a good value proposition.

This dream was soon to be a reality. I was given an opportunity of setting up an office in the Empire State building. And, an IT consulting company owned by an expat Indian offered me a corner cubicle space in his plush office on the 14th floor of the Empire State Building.

Life couldn't get any better. I was visiting The America's because I was invited by the congressmen themselves. By then, there were approximately 40,000 users in my mailing list and a majority of them were IT workers already present in The Americas. Being the founder of a knowledge worker organization, it would have been an opportunity to find synergy and any corporate with a vision of being socially responsible could see value in supporting the NOSTOPS cause. I believed this could have been the reason for the generosity!

It was 9pm and snowing outside and the view from the 14th floor office atop the Empire State Building was breathtaking. The Hudson River was all silver and reflected bright with New Jersey's night skyline. I had just arrived from my dinner and was perched on the desk hacking away the day's events on my blog and announced the setting up of the new telephone helpline number 1-800 H1-BHELP to the members of my mailing list. I hit the enter key on keyboard and sent out the newsletter to the mailing list. Within the hour, I began receiving calls on the new number. Calls came in from members congratulating me on the successful launch of the helpline.

In the hour I spoke with, I received calls from Toronto, Barbados, California, Austin, Texas, Dubai and even from India. As I greeted every caller, I also quizzed them on the local time. I was speechless. The IT Company CEO had indeed been supportive and extremely helpful in donating NOSTOPS these 2 phone numbers. I had given them due credit in my mailings as well as on the blog.

After hanging up on my last phone call at about 1 am, that night, I stepped out of the office on the 14th floor, took the elevators down stairs for a last smoke before I called it a day. The day one was fruitful.

As I looked around, I observed the restaurants were wide open. Quite a few of these restaurants were open 24 x 7. Watching late night tourists walking in and out of these restaurants was a pleasant feeling. I compared my NOSTOPS with the 24 x 7 business operation in front of me.

As I stubbed the cigarette butt, I smiled – mine was a transnational operation. And my callers were calling from out of the United States as well. Tomorrow, I was positive I'd be receiving a lot of phone calls and NOSTOPS would embark on its real journey – of facilitating issues of knowledge workers.

Indeed the next morning was eventful; it began with receiving tons of emails - some congratulating me, other seeking my help and an appointment to speak with me over the telephone. I replied to each and every email that I had received in response to my last night's mail. I set up appointments and scheduled my time so that I could dedicate 15 minutes to every caller. I had scheduled 11 phone meetings – not bad for day two!

It was 8:45 am, and I had my first scheduled caller at 10 am. Enough time for a quick nap, before the employees of the IT firm arrived. I slept at my desk only to wake up close to noon. I checked my emails and waited for the next scheduled caller to call in. I received no calls whatsoever. I was terribly dejected. I knew my members would never fail me and I was looking forward to receiving their calls.

As I narrated the challenges to one of the colleague sitting across my cubicle, he dialed the toll free helpline number. He spoke briefly, and hung up his cell phone. He then burst out in a shrill laugh that was terribly annoying I still remember, it must have been a full two minutes before I could expect him to answer.

He looked at me with a calm pathetic look on his face and said – "your calls are routed to a call center in Hyderabad in your country!"

The CEO of the IT firm had simply without my permission routed calls to his call center in Hyderabad!" NOSTOPS members were solicited and sold into recruitment without their or my knowledge.

5 pm the following day, I was at the waiting lounge at the JF Kennedy airport -heading back to India. As I was speaking with Donna, thanking her for her efforts and generosity in inviting me and making possible the dream of visiting Capitol Hill. I then went on explaining to her the 'deal' about the helpline; and how I was conned into believing corporate support; we laughed and laughed over the telephone like teenagers sharing a good joke. The next couple of hours spent in solitude were heartwarming. I was heading back to India after a fruitful two months. It was just a matter of time now that the United States government would be doing its part and begin scratching off the paint of the masks of scamsters. I left Uncle Sam with a heavy heart!

Consistently throughout the past 10 years, Indian companies with head offices in India were the highest users of the H1-B, L-1 visas. Employees of these giants, traveling on business visas too, were in high numbers. Companies that were required to pay a salary on the H1-B visa, including the time the sponsored H1-B worker was without a job (benching provisions), found the L-1 visas (the intra company managers on rotation) a convenient way to avoid the requirement of paying a salary, and get away by paying an allowance. The increased profits, of companies having head offices back in India, were transferred back making huge real estate investments. In

India, a real estate purchase is usually not transparent. A majority of the purchase is made in cash.

Upon my arrival back in India, in the following few months, Senators Durbin & Senator Grassley, authors of the "H1-B and L-1 Visa Fraud and Abuse Prevention Act of 2007" bill proposal, sent out letters to 9 Indian IT companies, those that requested H1-B petitions for its employees in large numbers, questioning them about the way they use the H1-B visa program.

Dated May 14th, 2007, the letters were sent out to Mphasis Corporation, Tech Mahindra Americas, Inc, I-Flex Solutions, Inc, Larsen & Toubro InfoTech Limited, Patni Computer Systems, Satyam Computer Systems Limited, Tata Consultancy Services Limited, Wipro Limited, and Infosys Technologies Limited.

The letters written to the CEO's of these companies, read as below –

Dear Sir,

As Members of the Senate Judiciary Committee Subcommittee on Immigration, Border Security and Refugees, we have a responsibility to oversee and evaluate our country's visa policies. We have been concerned about the reported fraud and abuse of the H1-B and L visa programs, and their impact on American workers. We are also concerned that the program is not being used as the congress intended.

While some Members of Congress have focused on increasing the annual cap of the H1-B program, we believe it is important to understand how the H1-B visas are used by companies in the United States. We have received helpful data from the U.S Citizenship and Immigration Service with regard to the H1-B visa approvals in 2006 for the top 200 participating companies. Your company was one of the top companies on the list. Therefore, we are requesting your cooperation in providing additional statistics and information on your use of H1-B visa workers.

First, some groups, such as the Programmer's Guild, have analyzed the wages paid to H1-B visa holders. They have found that the average annual salary of foreign workers is significantly lower than that of new U.S graduates.

Second, a number of consulting firms reportedly recruit foreign workers and then outsource the individuals to other job sites or companies. Many of the top 20 companies that used H1-B visas in 2006 are firms, such as yours, that specialize in off shore outsourcing.

Third, a number of firms have allegedly laid off American workers while continuing to employ H1-B visa holders. The American people are concerned about such layoffs at a time when the demand for visa issuances and the recruitment of foreign workers appear to be increasing.

Because of these concerns, we seek your cooperation in answering the following questions:

NUMBERS:

- How many United States citizens do you employ in the United States?
- Is your company an H1-B dependant employer?
- How many visa petitions did you submit to the Citizenship and Immigration Service for Fiscal Year 2007?
- Of the total number of petitions requested, how many have been approved for Fiscal year 2007, if known?
- How many H1-B visa holders is your company currently employing? What percentage of your total workforce are H1-B visa holders?
- What is the average age of the H1-B visa holders that your company currently employs?
- What is the average numbers of years of experience of your employed H1-B visa holders?
- Please describe your efforts to recruit Americans for the positions for which you employ H1-B workers

WAGES:

- What is the average wage of your company's H1-B visa holders? What is the median wage? What are the highest and

lowest salaries for those H1-B visa holders currently employed by your company?
- What is the average wage of your company's workers who are United States citizens in the same occupations?

OUTSOURCING:

- Of the XXX visas your company received in 2006, how many of those workers are currently employed and paid by your company?
- Of the XXX visas your company received in 2006, how many were outsourced to other companies and how many employees' salaries were paid for by a fir other than your company?

LAYOFFS:

- Has your company experienced any layoffs in the United States in the past year? Any layoffs in 2005? If so, how many people lost their jobs?
- If your company has laid off workers in the United States, what positions were part of that lay off?
- If your company has laid off workers in the United States, how many of those workers were H1-B visa holders?
- If your company has laid off workers in the United States, did any H1-B visa holders replace those dislocated workers, or take over any of the laid off employee's job responsibilities?

We appreciate your cooperation, and respectfully request that you respond to our questions no later than May 29, 2007

Sincerely,

Charles E. Grassley   Richard J. Durbin

United States Senator   United States Senator

The letters were sent out to companies as an attempt to question their intent and their usage of the visa quota. It also served as intent of the forth coming investigations. Ironically, in the months that followed, while a few companies were acquired under new leaderships, others minimized their visa usage of their employees. But a few others continued the visa misuse.

I must confess, in my eagerness to bring about decorum, I have been naïve in my approach. It has been a trial and error method that I have put to use while communicating with the Indian IT corporate. Some have gotten me into trouble, some have caused me embarrassment, and in some instances, I have been offered money – large sums of it!

I once needed to negotiate an important cross border immigration related aspect with a potential significance of high repute. I had recently testified in the US Congress against the misuse of work visa programs by corporations heavily dependent on Indian workers. And so this meeting was pre-ordained, immediately upon my arrival in Bangalore.

An official at the company I was dealing with demanded that I meet with the spouse of the company CEO and offer an at length account of what the forthcoming actions would be under taken by the US Department Of Justice against companies such as theirs. The confidence meeting ended with a generous offer of Rs 10 lakhs, offered as a gesture of support towards my knowledge worker centric organization that I was building ground up.

In return I was to give the spouse stock in my organization in return for their support. A stock gift could have led to millions in sales. If I declined, I would lose the business opportunity and the much needed capital to jump start our day-to-day operations and help me personally with the much needed cash, while I was undergoing a divorce trial in the local family courts of Mumbai.

I was totally dumbfounded. In other parts of the world, propositions like this one are common business practice. But this was happening to me when I was fighting against companies such as these, those that were affecting workers at large – I wasn't willing to compromise!

I decided that I would rather sink my organization rather than compromise my values. I declined the deal.

Our team was forced back to the drawing board to develop new avenues. Eventually we built our organization without their support and went on to become an organization with a million plus members today. And we were able to get the support from not only the workers themselves, but from the media across borders as well.

I believe, the key to achieving success is in laying a strong foundation based on ethical merits. Over the ten years, we did a great job in communicating the issues that hurt - not just about the workers issues but social issues as well that put the society in a conundrum. When the determination is strong, I felt one should never have the need to compromise on ethics. For instance, having zero tolerance to corruption and refusing to pay a bribe to win over someone to our side.

On the personal front, I had to simply let go the opportunity of seeking visitation rights to my daughter because I was unwilling to bribe anyone. This was hard to do and it hurt because I couldn't disclose what happened. But it was the right decision to make for the long term. I survived and if I had not made this decision, I would not have been inspired to work harder over the years. If I had accepted to offer stock to the spouse of the CEO of one of the largest software services company today, I would have been rich, and possibly even had the opportunity to be united with my family, but then it would have cost me of living with the guilt, and my reputation. I could never live up to that.

Neither would I have enjoyed repeatedly reading in the media about the malpractices of the same company whose cash support I had declined.

8 JUSTICE DELAYED, JUSTICE DENIED

During those struggling days, one could easily attract high net worth individuals to work with, especially at a time when the organization often spoke on certain worker issues through the media. All you had to do was to make sky-high projections for growth, say you were in the cross border knowledge worker migration space and then just go along with their unscrupulous agenda of 'bodyshopping'.

A few early business partners wanted me to do just that; what many other successful CEO's had done and go full on being a body shopper on the side, to fuel our cash flow. But I was worried that I would be misleading the public and filling my company's coffers with the savings of unsuspecting parents and struggling families.

To them a public presence seemed like a confirm bet to rake in big money, and then walk away, and disown responsibilities for the company's projections. The public were the losers. I chose not to continue with such business partners and allowed them to resign eventually. Weeding out the bad apples, so that just the best values and ethics stayed in organization has been an ongoing process.

Eventually, the media did begin reporting the illegality and crack down of the body shopping businesses and defamed many companies. Reports of many families losing their savings were being reported. Most of the companies that went public also ceased to exist.

When I think back, I know I could have made tens of millions of dollars and lived the high life. But I would never have felt right about spending this money. I would not have been able to face the people whose money I was spending. I would not have been able to live with myself.

Turning away from the lakhs of rupees with a purported agenda was the best decision I ever made.

While the worker issues specific to the employer abuses were communicated and the loopholes were being fixed, the pro migration agenda of workers going overseas continued. In an article published in August of 26th, 2009, on rediff.com, a leading portal then for non resident Indians, I sought the reader's attention to look at the pitfalls of seeking employment overseas by falling prey to scamsters. The article offered advice to the job seeker on how to source employment overseas, and how to identify a fraudulent job offer. It also cautioned them from being aware of the received job offers and to be extremely careful of employer contracts. Cautioning the job seeker to be aware of the underground economy where email addresses were harvested by unscrupulous individuals. The article was aptly renamed by the editors – "Want a job overseas? Beware of Fraud."

Around the same time, in California, social immigrant's rights activist David Bacon published a book titled "Illegal People: How Globalization Creates Migration and Criminalizes Immigrants" and speaks extensively of the Pitfalls of using Immigration as a labor supply system for employers. He hosts a weekly radio show on KPA-FM in Berkley, California.

In his book, David traces the development of the illegal immigrant status back to slavery and shows the human cost of treating the indispensable labor of millions of immigrants. Through the book, he argues for a change in the way we think debate and even legislate around the issues of migration and globalization – making a compelling case for why we need to consider immigration and migration from a globalized human rights perspective. Citing many examples of the Mexican Oaxacan farming families to the present day high skilled workers and low salaries, he has made a connection of the modern day work visa programs with that of the historic slavery in Americas.. He has made numerous references to me as well as my organization addressing issues specific to the modern day guest worker programs.

In one of his live weekly show "Black, Brown and White together", in which I too participated telephonically, he asked the listeners - Should the U.S immigration rest on managing the labor flow or be more focused on the human rights of its workers?

Coincidentally it may be worthwhile to note that, the year the modern day H1-B guest worker program began, the UN Convention was also adopted in 1990. The UN Convention extends the basic human rights to all migrant workers and their families - legal or illegal. And supports family reunification, establishes the principle of equality of treatment with citizens of the host country in relation to employment and education; protects migrants against collective deportation and makes both the countries that send and receive workers responsible in protecting their workers' rights.

On the personal front, it had already been more than 3 years since I last saw my daughter and I was making repeated attempts at the local family court seeking visitation access. Needlessly, the corruption in the courts was prohibiting me from even filing my petition. I must have spent close to 10 weeks, just attempting to file a petition seeking visitation access – basically, it was an attempt to simply see my daughter.

I remember, I had enthusiastically approached my in-laws, to share with them, the good news with proof of the visa draft and that I personally visited the US Congress and met with those people who had the capacity to make changes to the visa program. I wanted to share that I had met the US Congressmen in person and shook their hands, I had explained to them how it had affected me and my family and I had proof that not only they listened to what I had to say; the changes were being made and a new law was soon going to be in implemented.

It was my attempt to show to my in-laws, that the hurt I indirectly caused my wife was not my fault alone, but it was due to the broken system. And I had spent the past couple of years trying to be heard and I had been successful in my efforts. I wanted to hand deliver personally, the sixty eight pages of the forthcoming visa draft of the reform bill.

Yet again, unfortunately for me, this time around the abuses were even stronger. I was abused verbally and called a dog that kept coming back again and again. Things were getting too out of control. Here I was, I spent the past few years not knowing anything of my dearest ones. I had kept quiet in the courts, allowing her to win. Instead I spent the years, trying to bring merit to my cause by promising to deliver upon the misconstrued allegations. And now, I was shooed away.

Father's Need Their Children Too

As a divorced dad, I am continuing to struggle with a fact that so many people refuse to accept – that fathers play a unique and an irreplaceable role in their children's lives. Despite the studies and research data available, there are those that believe fathers are replaceable—that father's simply fulfill a role that any other man or even a woman can fulfill. If this were true, cocky deadbeat men would just sow their wild oats and simply walk out of their marriages!

Over the years, I have also been confronted by many, who believe that another man can replace a child's father, and the resulting conclusion a majority have reached, for me, is that dads are dispensable. While I continue to believe that fathers are indispensable, I have tried to look deeper in my reasoning to understand why so many people ignore this fact and the common sense – that fathers are NOT replaceable.

I was yet again part of a larger problem – young innocent children caught between disputing parents. I knew there were many fathers like me, who sought access to their children. Some have been fighting for many years. There were many like me who had returned back to India and re settled, leaving everything they had permanently.

I met a couple of father's like me, who were unable to meet their children, and then there were many others – someone who knew someone else in similar situations. Taking action, a small group of seven, would meet up at a coffee shop after work and share our challenges and the social stigma attached and to discuss how rampant the corruption was.

We didn't know if fathers elsewhere in the country were facing the same challenges. We did know though, the family laws were addressed differently as the culture lies at the root of how the divorce cases were perceived. Because India is a land of diversity, local customs and conventions that are not against any particular statute or morality or otherwise undesirable, were also recognized and taken into account by the courts while they administered justice in certain spheres. Also, people of different religions and traditions were governed by different sets of personal law with respect to matters relating to family affairs.

In February 2009, we began an online group called "Children in the Centre" (CITC). The purpose of the group was for fathers seeking visitation rights to come together and communicate a common message while their litigation was in process. The message was simple and clear – it was a call for 'disputing parents to come together as consenting adults'. We came together collectively so that we could ask the judiciary to look at a child's basic need to be loved by both the parents.

When the media took notice to the plight of fathers like us and gave our group some great coverage, the responses from others throughout the country were overwhelming. The challenges faced by fathers distanced from their children were overwhelming. Some related the never ending saga of spousal abuse; others narrated the catastrophic damage caused in their children's lives due to the years of separation. It did not take much consensus to assess that the psychological effects on the father's and their children's lives were completely ignored by the judiciary.

On September 9th, 2009, at 11 am I was walking the corridor of the Prime Minister's Office in New Delhi. I was walking towards the mail room of the PMO. I was advised to submit a formal application stating my 'ask' from the government. I wrote the following letter, addressed to the Honorable Prime Minister, and attached to it, the same mornings article that spoke about our group "Children in the Center". My letter to the PM was as follows -

To,

The Honorable Prime Minister,

Prime Minister's Office,

New Delhi

Subject: Keeping Children in the Center and focusing on their welfare

Honorable Sir,

In lieu with the discord with respect to the family disputes at the civil family courts in Bandra, Mumbai; I'd like to put on record my failure to give justice to my only child, now aged 11 years, due to the inability to prevent myself from succumbing to the corruption and nepotism in the family court proceedings.

As a returning Non Resident Indian, I have been seeking visitation rights to my only child which has been denied repeatedly. My daughter is unwell and I am denied access and every possible effort has been turned down, including my right to receive my child's school grades and now her health reports as well as the knowledge of her whereabouts have been denied.

I am not alone in this fight for justice, of a father fighting for justice in wishing to meet his own child. We have formed a group of father's, fighting our tears and our fears of losing our children forever.

Attached herewith is today morning's recent newspaper article that speaks of our group and may serve as evidence of our participation to the cause. I'd be obliged to seek a point of contact to best explain the issues that prohibit effective governance and eliminate the rampant corruption in the courts of law. Also attached are some emails of those in similar or worst conditions - of parents in distress.

I'd like to be able to make a presentation to the officials and those concerned on the need to accommodate our children's need to be loved by both parents and not subject them to hatred in their innocent years. An intervention from your office is highly warranted. Towards the well being of our children, the future citizens, an expedited effort from your office is sought in earnest. .

In anticipation and hope,

Signed Rajiv Dabhadkar

Soon after, when I once again petitioned seeking visitation access to my daughter, I was granted access for one full hour, once a year, on my daughter's birthday. But for making this access possible, I had to make an application to the courts exactly a month in advance of my child's birth day. The court would then receive response from my child's guardians and then the place of visit would be decided. To further know the place of the visit, I had to approach the courts not before a week before the birth day.

Completely frustrated, I gave up! Between me and my daughter - I always wondered who the bigger criminal was, and why we both were punished. Ever since the decision, I did not find any reasons to approach the courts knowing very well that any complete arbitration, if at all, was best achieved outside of the courts.

But as fate would have it ... there was to be a beginning to standing up and speaking for self and tell my end of the story. I was now more determined and deeply rooted to the cause.

On October 1st, 2009, a media campaign in the US, that included an investigation on fraudulent immigration practices by companies; lead to an in depth cover story in the Business week (New York City), titled - "America's High Tech Sweat Shops".

The efforts required bringing about the story out in the open. Eighteen members of NOSTOPS participated, and worked with the editors and reporters of the publication. The eighteen individuals, at that time were spread across the globe, and were in different countries, in different time zones altogether, but they were those that were affected in one way or the other by the scrupulous 'body shops' not too long ago.

The investigation by the team was progressing very well and each of the eighteen members had a story to tell. They were eager to speak of their stories – of being duped, abused and scammed.

To bring about a 360 degree balanced viewpoint to the news story, I fell upon a gentleman, for advice, who has been a renowned entrepreneur turned professor and was a globalization research expert, with a well funded foundation. The foundation studies the impact of globalization on American businesses. He was a celebrated globalization expert, and an author with a pro-immigration stance. He disagreed on my views on the volume of worker abuses and human rights violations that were specific to foreign workers on short term work visas. According to him, a handful of those affected, should not be the reason to scrutinize companies seeking foreign labor.

I considered him an authority on the subject. Someone who wrote extensive op-ed columns in international publications, I felt it was important to seek his opinion on the ramifications of the story that was been built. It was after all going to be a cover story, with a famous publication. I was leading the story, and there were a handful of people, those that belonged to my organization, that were willing to come forward and speak.

It was a sincere, innocent gesture in seeking his advice, but what came back was a rude shock, something that I was unprepared for, compelling me to reconsider my stance with respect to the cause that I was personally pursuing. I was questioned of my intent of what I was speaking to the media about. Was I self promoting my hurt and seeking attention? I was alleged to be creating a storm in a tea cup and did not realize the depth and the impact of the international coverage this would bring to the subject of fraud and abuse by companies with certain ethnic origins. I was accused of working with the other side and adding fodder to the xenophobic anti-H1-B visa sentiment. I was further blamed of having sold my soul and was accused of speaking to the media just for a ticket to America! If this wasn't sufficient, I was also questioned why I was dragging eighteen others and putting their lives at stake, by having them interviewed with the publication. I was shell shocked. And I was hurt.

Sure, I was personally hurt. But what happened to me was way back in 2001. And I have never made my personal issues known. Over the years, with the countless feedback I received; I had simply forged forward in generating awareness via the media. This time as well, I was making a sincere attempt, only because many members of my organization were hurt too. It just wasn't me alone anymore. With the transparency that allowed, I forwarded the accusatory email to all the twenty four concerned individuals - the editors, their reporters as well as the eighteen members, who were eagerly sharing their story – exposing the fraud, and the abuses. It had taken about eight weeks to create the cover story that included hard facts and evidences to support claims of victimization.

Surprisingly, everyone took ownership. A few of the eighteen that were interviewed, replied back with encouragement, asking me to have the courage to continue in doing what was right. The emails of support were simply overwhelming. Therefore, for the first time, I too came out with my own story. I came out with what had happened to me. My story came out as a surprise to many, especially friends and family back home. But, I did my due diligence to the cause. I was a naked man who was ever too willing to offer his shirt!

The story went to print and the online version was flashed globally via Reuters. It appeared not only in the American media, but also in Philippines, Mexico, United Kingdom, and Canada. Most importantly, for the first time, the Indian newspapers carried the story as well.

Now, one thing was certain - the issue wasn't just my own. It was evident now, that many were affected and many were coming forth with their story. As workers reported contractual breaches by their employers, claims seeking withholding of wages, reports of visa scams such as paying for a visa but never receiving it, arriving in the country with no job to go to, took the nay Sayers and the fence sitters by surprise. America's attempt to scratch the paint off the masks of fraudulent H1-B dependant employers had just begun.

We then began a series of awareness campaigns using the media and augmented issues one at a time. A piecemeal approach to tie down the loose ends, to restore the initial intent of 'good faith' hiring of the work visa programs had finally begun.

Subsequently on January 8th 2010, Donald Neufeld, Associate Director, Service Center Operations, of The United States Citizenship and Immigration Services, made public a memo - commonly known as the 'Neufeld Memo'. The memo officially declared what constitutes an H1-B Employer-Employee Relationship while considering the filing of H1-B petitions including the placement of foreign workers on third-party sites.

The purpose of this memo was to provide guidance in the context of H1-B petitions, on the requirement that a company filing the petition on behalf of its workers must show that the employer-employee relationship does exist and will continue to exist with its work visa sponsored employee throughout the duration their visa is valid.

The United States Citizenship and Immigration Services looked at many factors to determine if an employer-employee relationship exists, more than merely engaging a person to work in the United States and paying him the salary wage. It looks at whether the employer has a sufficient control over its employee. The right to control is established over when, where and how the employee performs such work. This is considered using any of the following factors-

- Does the employer supervise the employee and is such supervision on-site or off-site?
- If the supervision is off-site, how does is the supervision maintained – ie: weekly calls, reporting back to the main office routinely, or site visits by the employer?
- Does the employer have the right to control the work of the employee on a day-to-day basis if such control is required?
- Does the employer provide the tools or instruments needed for the employee to perform the duties of employment?
- Does the employer hire, pay and have the ability to fire the beneficiary?
- Does the employer evaluate the work / product or conduct progress/ performance reviews of the employee?
- Does the employer claim the employee for tax purposes?
- Does the employer provide the employee any type of employee benefits?
- Does the employee use any type of proprietary information of the employer in order to perform its employment duties?
- Does the employee produce an end product that is directly linked to the employer's line of business?

- Does the employer have the ability to control the manner and means in which the work product of the employee is accomplished?

The employer must establish that it has the right to control the employee's work through the employee's duration of employment. The memo goes further to establish some types of employment scenarios to show what constitutes existence of a valid employer-employee relationship.

Via this memo, the intent was clear, it was an attempt made by the government to define the conditions by which employers could seek new workers from overseas and / or request an extension on the work visas of their existing employees. It was an awareness drive by the government to educate the employers and serve as a justification to those employers whose visa petitions were declined.

Over the course of a couple of years, while the activity of awareness building proving evidences of fraud and abuse via the media has been a consistent effort, I became a whistleblower and encouraged others indentured to stand up to abuse and report complaints as well. While I facilitated queries of users that sought help against threats from their employers at goolti.com - a whistleblower web site, the growing investigations encouraged others to stand up and fight for their rights individually. And as the nationwide audit investigations revealed, the fraud was not limited to offshore companies alone, but local American firms as well.

9 STEPPING UP THE MANDATE

It was an interesting process, while the American media was eager to know how the foreign workers, a majority of those from India were treated with prejudice, they also wanted to know how the growing digital divide was affecting workplace rights of their own workers; the Indian media however did not seem to be interested! They simply chose to ignore their own worker woes, especially of those serving overseas. Indian media continued to ignore the plight of their own subjugated workers working overseas, but rather chose to write about the flamboyant lifestyles of the CEO's of the very same Indian companies.

The tipping point came about eventually, but until then, I have been turned down repeatedly. I believe the perception of me was of someone, who had been battered and was vengeful. I may have seemed to be having an anti-H1-B agenda, and was against Indian employers, because I was encouraging Indian workers to stand up against employer abuse – that I was asking Indian workers to seek better pay, better living conditions, and along with it all, a life of respect.

While it took media to get the message across;, I have many a times led media initiatives. Often, the media initiatives were specific to the migrant Indian workers overseas. Most of these were driven with an agenda of – creating awareness, bridging the gap, uniting both sides of worker classes and collectively addressing the need for change.

It was a difficult challenge. To get the right message across, working on different continents, and working with two different cultural mindsets, it was critically important to keep a balance between the inward as well as the outward migration happening in India and the United States. The message also had to be deeper. Just the fact that corruption and the brokerage of intellectual capital disrupt the labor market ecosystem was not enough. As I soon realized, the message often was not accepted well. Not only with the neo-rich with a body shopping agenda, but with the locals here as well.

Incidentally, I was engaged with at a leading law school in the city of Pune, some 100 kms west of Mumbai, and was part of a research study on migration. The study involved researching India's own migration history, the effects of migration on employment and aligning India to the globalization wave – specifically it was about India's talent moving westward.

It was an excellent opportunity to be working with well known academicians, in a prestigious law school, that housed the Dr Babasaheb Ambedkar Museum within its campus perimeter. Dr Babasaheb Ambedkar, the greatest visionary wrote the Constitution of India. It was indeed a privilege to be a part of this migration research team.

It may be difficult to state in brief, but it may suffice to go on record and say that the study, in about a few months ended abruptly. There was a massive inter-state migration issue brewing and the political right wingers were agitated. Forgetting the migration study was the only recourse, as the issue had already reached mainstream politics! There was large scale hysteria, and there were debates on national television. A 'right to a job' by the local residents was the central theme of the agitation.

May 1st every year, the State of Maharashtra celebrates its Labor Day. Since a few weeks of the closure of the migration study program, the sentiments of residents of the State had been accusing workers coming from a few northern states and alleged them to be taking their jobs away. The inter-state migration issues related to job displacement were heating up. Migrant laborers in cities were brutally attacked.

Often, the local youth from where I lived, felt me speaking in favor of the north Indian migrants. The point I was making was that in a globalized world, workers rights are fast disappearing. If a phone has parts made from forty odd countries how does one say it was 'manufactured' in just one place? Migrants coming into the city were not taking away their employment; but they were a part of the society building the ecosystem as entrepreneurs. They are fully aware that certain jobs were reserved only to the locals, yet they invested their time and resources and served the community around them.

At a local event, my casual opinion expressing equal employment opportunity rights turned ugly and I was a recipient of blows and kicks by three individuals who like me; belonged to the same state and spoke the same language. I was hospitalized with a swollen face, a dislocated shoulder and a fractured limb!

Pin pointing specific issues required to generate awareness of Indians working overseas, required media coverage. And that made me a whistleblower. Along with the attention, I was also the recipient of threats and physical abuse. Over the years I have had been roughed up repeatedly, at times requiring hospitalizations. Though this was the last of the seven similar incidences over the years, my parents constantly worried for my safety and advised me to go away.

Even though the broken bones healed quickly, the bruises took a long time to heal – especially the emotional ones. I was confronted yet again, between making a choice of meeting my daughter in the courts in about two months or going away. I elected to go to the United States; and avoid being in harm's way – for self or to my family.

A Strategic Partnership for Renewed Markets

Back in the United States, in June 2010, I lived in Jersey City, New Jersey. I rented a small room in a family home closer to the Jersey City Medical Centre, because I was advised regular physiotherapy treatment to heal and strengthen my broken bones. I visited Manhattan often. Calling upon old friends, old colleagues, including buddies at the Yellow Cab Company, when I myself drove a yellow cab while a student. In about three months, I had healed completely.

I was at the Ground Zero standing by the fenced perimeter of the construction site. I was visiting Ground Zero after a long time. As I stood holding the fenced perimeter looking at the construction below, I shook terribly. I recollected the events of the day this twin towers collapsed. As I recalled the aftermath of the incident, my eyes welled in tears. I recollected my last conversation with my manager and two colleague friends those went down with the building. I even went in to see the Empire State Memorial wall and even read a few familiar names there. I spend about an hour at the Ground Zero, wiping my tears.

Standing there the zeal to continue was once again afresh and I was enthusiastic about my new initiative that I was to begin shortly.

In a few days, I began an initiative that aimed to mobilize and transform the workforce by focusing on the need to change the perception of guest workers. This initiative was "A Strategic Partnership for Renewed Markets". It aimed to seek support from companies to partner with to bring about a vision of creating an open H1-B employment void of employee fraud, reduce the corporate expose to employee fraud and reduce corporate human resource's employee validation expense.

The initiative went on to identify areas of fraud with some statistics. There was a massive problem that was hurting US and India's businesses and its people. According to the Citizenship and Immigration Service's "2008 H1-B Benefit Fraud & Compliance Assessment," –

13% of all H1-B applications were fraudulent and 21% of H1-B dependant employers were in violation of U.S. Immigration law. The Dept Of homeland Security, had conducted a random sampling of data, and the findings of fraud were:

- The business processing H1-Bs did not exist as a corporate entity;
- The educational degrees or experience letters submitted were fraudulent;
- 55% of overall violations were a result of the job location not listed in the I-129;
- 27% of the H1-B beneficiary did not receiving the prevailing wage;
- 42% of Computer-related occupations having H1-B visas had technical violations;

- 46% of H1-B visa holders were born in India, and 25% of these were fraudulent;
- 20.7% of the overall H1-B populations were in direct violation of immigration law;
- 20,000 H1-B visa petitions may have some type of fraud or technical violation(s).

The initiative openly advocated on the need to – "PROMOTE INDIA: Qualify the Source, Own the T.A.R.P (Transparency, Accountability, Reliability and Professionalism)". It was an initiative to bring focus to the rampant document fraud that existed in the work visa petitioning process.

While the initiative was led, it was also the time to acknowledge the 20th anniversary of the H1-B visa program. The most famous of all work visa programs, the H1-B program had completed 20 years, and it was important to get market feedback and to understand the unemployment metrics of the guest workers present in the United States. There was a growing insecurity of the H1-B program and concerns of its closure, similar to what had happened to the Bracero Program was high amongst the Indian community

The series of interviews we conducted with the help of the editors of Computer World magazine in Washington DC published views and opinions of the workers on the 20th Anniversary of the H1-B program.

There was evidence of unemployed H1-B visa holders, and the Indian community were well aware of the 'status limbo / visa orphans' status that is specific only to the H1-B visa holders. But alarmingly evident was the fact that local body shops in their efforts to circumvent getting scrutinized were hiring those on the Business visas (B1) for short term assignments, and bypassing American as well as the unemployed H1-B visa holders already present in the Americas

These findings were alarming and gave rise to a series of other articles, including the one where five people, including NOSTOPS members tell their H1-B stories in their own words, ("H1-B Special

Report- Computer World H1-B: The voices behind the visa.").

There were other related topics covered in the article series as well, namely :

"H1-B at 20: How the 'tech worker visa' is remaking IT in America"; "The H1-B visa program turns 20 years old this month. Not everyone in IT is saying 'Best Wishes.' ", "The H1-B visa is such a heated topic, its impact on individual high-tech workers often gets lost in the debate."

As a large number of employees of Indian companies sought to transfer onto an American firm shortly on arrival, the high numbers of H1-B visa petitions made by these employers was therefore questionable. There were many web sites that advertised job openings targeting "H1-B or L-1 visa holders only", thus excluding American citizens to not being considered for these open positions. Within months, these ads on prominent job portals such as Dice.com showcased advertisements of employers making employment offers to "International students only". This preference to international students was a way to bypass and segregate the existing American workers as well as the guest workers on valid work visas. These advertisements were of serious concern when there was unemployment under the H1-B program including growing evidence of companies' not paying overtime and withholding salaries was at large.

At a time, when there was serious misuse of work visas, when companies were using other short term visas to bring in workers, there was an increase in the unverified job posts on career web sites. As the career sites were monitored, online job posts seeking those on F-1 and Occupational Practical Training (OPT) candidates were large in numbers. These ads bypassed local workers as well as the existing and unemployed guest workers already present in the United States.

It was important to find a connect between Indian companies sending workers to the United States on 'Knowledge transfer', and not 'Project work' (short term employment) with that of the growing unemployment of H1-B workers.

Because individuals on B-1/B-2 visa holders were sought by

employers, it was noted that, often in between employment, existing H1-B visa holders transferred their work visa status to short term business visas. This helped both the companies as well as their employers to avoid the scrutiny.

This time around, however, there was discontent amongst the companies that were dependant on the immigration policies. And American workers were angry. The advertisements that preferred workers on short term visas; were being excluded from competing in the job market.

Jack Palmer, an American knowledge worker filed a class action law suit lawsuit against Infosys, while a similar lawsuit was filed against Larsen & Tourbo InfoTech by their American employees. Large Indian corporations with head offices in India were accused of visa misuse and immigration fraud.

In January, 23rd 2011 an article in Live Mint newspaper titled "Misuse of US visas may be widespread" provided evidence of widespread misuse of visas not only by Indian owned firms but by American firms as well. Unfortunately, when the US Court in Alabama dismissed Jack Palmer's harassment suit, because the state of Alabama did not recognize whistleblower laws, it meant less power for foreign workers to speak against any abuses meted out to them against their visa sponsors, more so because American workers themselves could not receive the justice.

In the case of the Jack Palmer's lawsuit, technically speaking, the state of Alabama was not responsible for immigration law violations as these were governed by the federal laws. Some critics even said the age old Jim Crowe laws were still in effect in the state of Alabama. I went on record and my views and telephonic statement were recorded - on the ramification of the Alabama court's judgment not focusing on the plight of foreign guest workers. These were put on record in an article titled "US court dismisses Palmer's harassment suit against Infosys".

Promoting Circular Migration

Rampant scrutiny of staffing agencies was deterring the prospects of those with fraudulent agendas. There was a serious concern on the plight of those in a visa status limbo or the so called 'visa orphans', working for these companies. The growing unemployment amongst the guest workers because they were abandoned by their visa sponsors and companies preference to recruit fresh foreign international students on F-1 visas was creating a greater void. The iceberg was melting and there was an urgent need to bring back workers. And it had to be done by promoting a positive image of migration between US and India and create possibilities of their return back to India, even temporarily.

Incidentally, around the same time, Shine.com, a Hindustan Times led Initiative had scheduled a job fair to recruit workers in the United States; those that were looking forward to employment opportunities in India.

It was a good time to promote inclusive growth, that was not only specific to workers of Indian origin but also to accommodate foreign born nationals. This was a great value proposition and an opportunity to promote 'circular migration' as a concept, against the typical reverse brain drain, undermining the stigma of returning non resident Indians. The term 'circular migration' was chosen because it brought about an effective win: win in a globalized economy, where labor displacement; as a product of dislocation was an ongoing process.

With a need to getting a job quickly as possible, and promoting a healthy compete between America's worker class, the job fair was promoted in many American cities following EEO laws.

The article first appeared in the Computer World, on 11th of November 2011 and gave the much needed publicity with over 3,000 shares on social networking sites. "Looking for work? Here's a job fair touting tech openings in India", promoted the Hindustan Times initiative gaining a wider publicity in North America. A job fair that was open to American workers as well as to the returning Indian workers. It hoped to reduce the unemployment amongst the H1-B visa holders primarily.

Most importantly, it promoted not only the jobs back in India, the initiative sent a message of 'circular migration' as well. I also felt that the media had been using the term 'brain drain' too loosely, as a tool to provoke or instigate. However, it was important to move away from the naïve concept and to promote the concept of circular migration that focused on the labor displacement caused by the shift in economy globally.

Policy Changes – Stapling Green Card to International Students

While it was imperative, that America had a genuine need to retain the best and brightest, but it could not simply rely on foreign workers alone. It had to prioritize its own work force and train them to be employable. To make them employable required some changes. A change that would require removal of the condition of being tied to a visa broker, in a 'dual employment', and eliminating 'visa brokerage' that made workers less favorable due to their visa shunting. Needlessly, the focus on making an offer of permanent residency was therefore imperative, by making an offer of a fast track "Green Card" for students studying in American Universities.

A proposal by New York Senator Chuck Schumer, offers conditional provisions for International Students, by giving them priority in recruitment. International Students on the completion of their course work, and with a confirmed job offer could now qualify towards direct permanent residency and these applications will be handled in top priority. A separate 40,000 quota of Green Cards were to be allocated for this category alone.

With this proposal, the objective was clear - to give preference to those studied domestically against hiring fresh-off-the-boat workers, and making it difficult for employers to make lower prevailing wage claims in their Labor Application to the Department of Labor. The new proposal would therefore encourage education as a priority and in essence make the H1-B visa program less favorable.

But even though the work visas' broken system was getting fixed piece by piece; India was fast losing its cutting edge. Firms were using Indian workers, and herding them in large numbers. And Indian workers experienced serious unemployment. Companies that 'banked visas' just had to deploy their visa approved 'benched' employees' onsite. America was seriously concerned with the amount of fraudulent visa applicants.

As employers in India dependant on deploying its workers on-site to the Americas lobbied to ratify the United Nations Mode 4, seeking a reduction in the visa filing fees, it was definitely an indication that the American government wanted to deter employers with fraudulent agendas. It was certain that while forthcoming policies would make it difficult for companies to commit fraud, it would however make it even more apparent for foreign students to seek admissions in American universities.

But it wasn't just the companies committing fraud either. Fraud was unearthed in dodgy universities that invited fraudulent students making the admission process frivolous. There was serious abuse of the J-1 student exchange program. As fraud in other visa categories was unearthed, it was getting obvious; America was aiming towards a comprehensive overhaul of its immigration system, and tightening the loopholes.

A closer look at how International Students are being recruited by American Universities will prove instance of scams; similar to the scams of University Of Virginia and the Tri Valley College in California.

Foreign education consultants – what you need to know

While leading publications carried articles warning of the perils of Indian students left in the lurch by American universities, such as Tri Valley. It complained about dodgy university scams that affect foreign students abroad. Fair enough – those sort of bogus universities are annoying. And not all universities aim to cheat. But such articles bring attention to argue the fact that the brokerage of student enrolments by foreign universities creates a student enrolment grey market that mislead and misinform.

Arguably, the pursuit of a foreign degree and the pleasure of walking into an education counselor's office should be kept separate in the same way as church and state. And here, I couldn't disagree more.

Higher education is a costly affair, and most importantly the student's future depends on it. There are bigger costs when it comes to seeking admission to a university overseas. Many would agree, the costs towards a Masters degree program in India is generally about 30 – 40 per cent lower than the 'preferred destinations' abroad.

Now the most obvious question arises – Why? Because unlike in India, getting admitted to a foreign university is often facilitated by a 'consultant', earning them a high mark up simply for filling a seat in an institution of higher learning abroad, increasing the tuition costs – sometimes up to 40 per cent higher.

One of the things that matters most to me is that people should be themselves. No one should feel obliged to adopt a particular process or put on a status quo issue. So here is my suggestion: if you want to seek a foreign university program and are hell bent on it, do a due diligence check on the student counselor you meet next. Arm yourself with the knowledge that often the most 'preferred' universities are not necessarily the ones that suit your needs rather they could be the ones that offer a greater profit margin to the counselor.

Know that the tuition fees you pay to the foreign university, a percentage of these come back to the counselor that has helped you seek an admission!

Have you ever been to one of those all-day exhibitions where in you can simply walk-in and meet a foreign university official, and walk out with a 'Letter of Admission'. Exhibitions hosted by their Indian representatives usually held in fancy hotels?

Be very careful of marketing gimmicks that offer on the spot admissions. 'On the Spot' admissions offer a conditional admission. 'Conditions applied' is a marketing gimmick that offers no immediate value to the student. Instead, it is an offer made without a promise.

I believe many of the best things happen when prospecting and convenience are mixed – over a streamlined process, for instance. Must recruitment be conducted solely in such lavish grandeur to entice students? Why such extravagance at the indirect cost to students? Foreign universities often engage in enrolment drives overseas visiting many countries to source student enrolments and offer on-the-spot admissions. It is an offer made, when the offer actually does not exist. Well known and state funded universities do not have to go out and seek students for enrolment, only the lesser known ones do.

There are of course some interesting variations to how student enrolments happen – and it seems to me that on the whole it is just an exhaustive affair. But there's a deep routed effect to these practices – students often end up paying admission fees to multiple foreign universities in the hope of getting a confirmed seat and consequently are recipients of multiple (I-20) immigration documents, allowing them to switch to a different college on arrival. God forbid if the university turns out to be a fraudulent one!

We cannot afford another Tri Valley or UNVA scam where hundreds of students get duped and are stranded jeopardizing their immigration status. Can the process of prospecting and recruiting for student's enrolments are done otherwise?

India has great universities too from which many Americans could benefit. Not only is the cost of an education in America very high but Americans as well as foreign students are taken advantage of by mediocre schools. If the great schools of India worked just as hard to get American students to come to India as India's students work to get into American schools, the playing field might be leveled for a number of reasons. Just as the Indian student who is (partly) educated outside India constitutes a member of an elite so does the American student who has a degree from a school in India. All things being equal, most American employers would give the advantage to such a student, who has demonstrated possibly better academic achievement than if he had attended some mediocre school in America, along with a more worldly and creative outlook. The question of English would benefit as well. A large group of Americans in India's classrooms will greatly help neutralize language/accent barriers (in both directions) to the benefit of all, regardless of where they end up working after graduation (many Americans working in America still work with Indians every day and of course vice versa).

Collective Voice – Boycott for Change

There seems to be a common ground of fraud and corruption when recruiting students or workers from India. Both common grounds point to the middlemen induced greed. While the host nation is concerned with the quality of its migrants, the sender country should be responsible to stem corruption at its source. Shouldn't that be the ideal partnership?

I believe the best way to walk the talk was to forge partnerships that had a common ground to come together. A common ground for likeminded organizations to come together as one and be vocal. In retrospect, my organization, NOSTOPS eventually partnered with three American tech advocacy groups, Bright Future Jobs, Programmers Guild, and Washtech and announced a professional labor boycott against companies such as Manpower, IBM and Infosys, because these companies regularly showed a pattern and practice of excluding US workers from job openings on US soil. NOSTOPS also supported them in their boycott.

Our joint Press Release said that the boycott will continue until these companies demonstrate employment practices that follow Equal Employment Opportunities (EEO) laws prohibiting race, gender, age and national origin discrimination for upcoming jobs in Fiscal Year 2016.

A report was released simultaneously, "Hidden Abroad: Manpower's Want Ads Revealed 'No Americans Need Apply' For Upcoming Jobs In Fiscal Year 2015." It revealed that Manpower Group commenced recruiting 7 months ago to exclude qualified U.S. technical professionals from jobs that will not be starting for another 6 to 10 months.

In a statement, Donna Conroy, Director of Bright Future Jobs and author of the 'Hidden Abroad Report' explained, "Most Americans believe the nature of the tech industry is so fast-paced that staffing projections cannot be adequately foreseen. However, these Manpower ads illustrate that U.S. tech employers determine labor needs 1-1.5 years ahead. This gives them plenty of time to seek Americans first. This boycott, combined with educating technical professionals on Equal Opportunity and other employment laws, will force the industry to change their ways."

Indian employers showed a strong preference for local talent for jobs in India, and I wondered why didn't these companies in the U.S. did the same? Partnering and supporting these three American tech worker organizations, I believed would protect the Indian foreign workers in the United States from the accusation of displacing Americans. Indians were not put on this earth to displace Americans, but Manpower's recruiting efforts did show this was their plan. This kind of segregated recruiting encourages unscrupulous agents to advertise jobs that do not require any specific technical skills and poach innocent Indian workers, making false promises.

The report analyzed Help Wanted ads posted on an Indian job portal, Naukri.com, between October through December 2013 by Manpower Group's wholly owned subsidiary, Experis IT India. These jobs wouldn't start until October 2014 through March 2015 in the U.S. The want ads targeted potential foreign workers and offered new H1-B visas. However, the ads stated a preference for those with U.S. experience and those who had successfully received work visas in the past.

These ads on Indian portals excluded not only the American citizens but also those with only an Indian experience.

These ads offered positions at "any of the experis delivery centers (Portland/Virginia/Michigan) or any of the client locations in the USA." Three rounds of interviews would start in November 2013; "2 rounds will be from US." One ad explained, "Experis will send a conditional offer letter which will be tentatively by end of March ("subject to visa approval" will be mentioned in that letter)." Those hired "would be expected to relocate to USA anywhere between October 2014 – march 2015."

All ads stated successful candidates would be working for Experis North America and "all expenses related to your visa filing would be taken care by manpower." Indian job seekers, in India, were assured that "Manpower Group would be filing for your H1-B visa by April, 2014."

I strongly believed that allowing the American citizens; the right to a job first, would protect the Indian foreign workers from the accusation of displacing Americans, and end the xenophobia against Indian workers. In retrospect, the Indian foreign workers could then seek help from their American Colleagues against abuses meted by their visa sponsors while working in The Americas.

This press release went online on June 2, 2014 and was covered by 46 news channels in 6 countries by June 6th, confirming the belief that workers across borders sought relief from corruption and recruitment fraud. The boycott was a clear indication of the intent to bridge the gap between local as well as foreign workers. It was "a call for attention", to restore Equal Employment Opportunity.

While the American tech advocacy groups sought inclusive hiring for jobs on their soil, The National Organization for Software and Technology Professionals (NOSTOPS) in India sought to bring attention to the entrapment of foreign workers due to labor bondage and brokerage of their salaries, identified as a prime reason for their lowered salaries. The foreign guest workers, however had other reasons for the boycott as well –

- America's 'Staffing only' firms, can also sponsor a work visa for a citizen from abroad. In terms of recruitment, the term 'employer' therefore is ambiguous and misleading for a worker in India, to whom the complexities of 'dual employment' overseas are largely unknown.

- American Work Visa sponsors bind their sponsored employee via elaborate employment contracts, prohibiting them the freedom to find work elsewhere.

- The Brokerage of Intellectual Capital drove down wages, and foreign guest workers are often underpaid. Multiple layers of broker agencies, that earn a per hour commission of their visa sponsored employee creates a grey market. Large scale grey market with invisible recruitment happening online to poach workers in India is a growing concern.

- America's work visas are used for temporary labor and very few sponsored guest workers gain permanent residency. No data on the H1-B work visa petitions converted to Green Card is available with the government.

- American employers gain competitive advantage and profitability by labor arbitrage - by paying low to their sponsored workers, and bidding high to their clients. Local workers are thereby, excluded from the job market. Importing foreign workers to make them a commodity and using them as products of labor violates their human rights.

- Experienced foreign guest workers already present in The Americas and those that need to be paid the prevailing wage at par with their gained American work experience, are replaced by fresh-off-the-boat new hires. Unemployed and benched experienced guest workers therefore are at alarmingly high numbers.

- Because of binding employment contracts by companies, employees abandon their employers upon arrival into The Americas. Companies therefore request visa petitions in large numbers and 'bank' visas. Approved work visa holders sitting in India looking for a job in The Americas is evident via online discussion boards.

Would the visa lottery thereby prove the existence of such banking of visas that exclude India's experienced freelance workers from being petitioned for visas by American firms directly?

A vast majority of American companies that advertise for local jobs on Indian career sites and Linked in groups are in the temp staffing arena where they don't have jobs but attempt to fill their client's jobs. This being a very competitive space, the company that can submit the most qualified candidates are likely to then receive approval from the client to place one or more of these workers. In essence, the temp staffing agencies need a wider pool of qualified candidates to present to their clients.

These temp staffing companies rely heavily on their good reputation among technical professionals to agree to be submitted for a potential contract. Because they are in the business of attracting foreign workers for a potential sale to their client companies in their country, it becomes very important for workers to arm themselves with a credible professional portfolio.

With the recent boycott to end employment discrimination via such fraudulent want ads, the competition for the H1-B visa will be even fiercer as companies have already begun seeking H1-B visa applications for FY 2016.

As the February 2014 article in Global Post- "Indian Hustle: How Fraudsters Prey on Would-be US Tech Workers" reported - "While there's little evidence that the Indian government has pursued the matter, in the US federal officers have had some success in fraud investigations over the last few years. Efforts to deal with the problem in India are limited. Data on attempted visa fraud are not collected by the Indian Government or any of the bodies that represent tech companies.

US officials in India make regular reports about fraudulent attempts to get visas. These are not ordinarily published, but Wiki leaks released a 2009 paper titled "India Semi-Annual Fraud Update."

At the time, according to the report, the vast majority of fraudulent applications came from the southern city of Hyderabad. Officers investigated 150 companies in the city and discovered that 77 percent "turned out to be fraudulent or highly suspect."

Officials uncovered a scheme where workers from Hyderabad were claiming to work for made-up companies in Pune so the Mumbai consulate would be less suspicious about their applications. "The Hyderabadis claimed that they had opened shell companies in Bangalore because 'everyone knows Hyderabad has fraud and Bangalore is reputable,'" according to the internal communiqué.

Will an Open Registry Arrest Labor Fraud?

So whether it is a job seeker that needs to verify an employment offer made by a foreign employer or the recruiter overseas that questions job seekers professional experience in India, the continued challenge lies in allowing the best match to happen between two sides that are saturated with fraud. How best can we restore Equal Employment Opportunity yet keeping open the doors to immigration?

Keeping stride with the economic benefits caused by labor displacement in a fast paced global economy, I believe, minimizing our exposure to fraud lies at the root of the debate on labor mobility. I believe, the answer lies in creating an open transparent system where workers are sought by employers globally, against them being pushed by the greedy corporate.

Imagine an open transparent repository of skilled workers that are clean, verified, and void of broker fraud. Imagine a flawless transition in bondage free employment contract with wages paid equal to or above the local wages that are in lieu with the rule of the foreign land.

Can we continue to fantasize on behalf of foreign employers participating in such an open employment that is void of employee fraud? Could an open registry of verified worker profiles therefore be the solution?

As the demand for workers and students will increase, the process of supplying this demand in the shortest possible time will therefore be imperative. It is therefore crucial to create an open transparent system where workers will be sought rather than pushed to employers globally. It is imperative therefore to create a registry of a verified workforce, workers whose education as well work experience is verified.

With the growing technological innovation aimed at an individual, the free movement of individuals is an arrived need. The accelerating globalization induced displaced labor in the labor markets that showed redundancies or labor sinks, created employment opportunities that needed to be filled in the shortest time period.

There were approximately well over 40 million individuals that still retained their Indian nationality and were serving in foreign destinations. This migrant population is set to accelerate further at an alarming pace; and social issues specific to these frequent traveling migrant community will increase as well. Circular migration therefore will increase the entrepreneurial capabilities of individuals that are inter- dependent on the foreign countries of residence. Creation of employment opportunities therefore will be obvious.

A growing registry of knowledge workers bring a wealth of information not only to the business community, thereby bridging the gap while overseas, but also aim to facilitate the ease in entry and exit procedures for individuals without being beholden to their employers. While hiring managers alleged that workers often smudge their employment profile, to compete for jobs, hiring an employee without a verified employment history delayed the hiring process as well as incurred heavy costs to the company.

The reason behind the Open Registry therefore was the belief that every knowledge worker should – Be motivated enough to be transparent, accountable, reliable and professional and to be sought rather than be pushed for employment. The open registry aims to offer the knowledge worker with the right toolsets to self serve his/her needs to be able to justify his/her earned overseas work experience as a 'returnee worker' or allow him/her to eliminate agent dependency while sourcing employment anywhere

While the workers have a consistent need to gaining employment opportunities either domestically or overseas it was also important for them to bring a competitive edge just so they were paid the optimum wage level,

But then, globally employers to have a need to - Find relevant candidates most suitable for immediate hire, by accessing and connecting with a global, on-demand workforce. The employers will be able to choose candidates whose professional credentials and work history details have been verified. The employers, irrespective of their geographic location will therefore hire the best candidate at the shortest time period; thereby minimize their dependency on outsourcing their recruitment needs. To an employer there is tremendous cost savings in lateral recruitment by participating an open employment that is void of employee fraud, thus reducing the companies expose to employee fraud and reduction, if not total elimination of the companies human resource related employee validation expense

It was time therefore; to create a system that not only gave value to an individual worker but also of a system that was dependable for employer's needs. A repository of workers that were clean, verified, and void of fraud, therefore was the greatest need. The idea was to not make it a closed system, rather make it a transparent worker repository of Education and Work Experience Verified Open Registry.

An Open Registry of verified knowledge workers sought by the employers globally will truly facilitate the domestic worker's transition overseas. Keeping it a truly open model that promotes India's best and the brightest talent globally.

In August 2010 the United Kingdom Border Agency, once again cited our press release "NOSTOPS launches Indiaverified.com to curb document fraud.", giving the initiative the much required credibility.

Solidarity in a global labor market

"If you come only to help me, you can go back home. But if you consider my struggle as part of your struggle for survival, then maybe we can work together" – These are the echoing sentiments of local workers globally.

Today, working people of India are participating in a continuing global economy. The borders that once separated them have now become common ground where workers and their families can come together and are no longer lines that separate them and pulled them apart.

Indian workers worldwide are forced into a global labor market and these workers have a direct interest in helping workers in other countries and in other cultures, to organize and to raise living standards; all in support of a free trade system. Not only that, working people also have a great advantage in the global economy by creating a human bond that connects them with other workers in countries of the developed and the developing world.

Some thoughts that come to my mind are:

* Which natural vehicle for solidarity is available then, other than knowing more about the working conditions in both halves of the world?

* Who can see most clearly the operation of the global economy, and have a greater stake in changing it?

Speaking of the on-site deployment of workers overseas, or the off shoring of jobs back home, it may justify the creation of employment opportunities. However, the arrangements made by these employers are inadvertently questioned, because somewhere in the process the human rights of their workers are violated. Those that happen subtly across borders.

Why? Because, when we consider globalization and the related job displacement it causes, it invariably pits one class of worker with the other – the citizens as well as guest workers, those with small, insecure incomes, who are in the same boat and appear to be fighting on the same side for better pay and better living conditions.

It may seem as though the global economy today has turned job insecurity into a virtue, convincing it as a necessary attribute to increase flexibility and competitiveness in the workplace. However, while evaluating proposals for immigration reform – security, equality, family and community are the watch words used by human rights activists. And any proposals that deny people their rights or benefits because of their visa status moves away from equality.

Reading what the recent media reports speak, it is but obvious that a change is sought by both sides and a new wave of reforms is therefore inevitable. Now, questions arise on how the forthcoming immigration proposals will align to the futuristic globalization needs of nations? Will one nation suffer at the cost of the other? Will the forthcoming change continue to tie guest workers to their foreign employers or will the workers be bound to one another instead, creating a never ending stream of migrant pool of happy working people?

Contrary to what the word on the street is, below are a few highlights of the forth coming 'Comprehensive Immigration Reforms', under which the US government will -

(1) Increase the annual quota to import foreign workers to 110,000 from the previously set 65,000, additionally a separate 25,000 quota reserved for those with a US education degree and want to return back to work. In future years, this quota can increase up to 180,000.

(2) Prevent foreigners on work visas from under cutting the wages paid to American workers by requiring employers to pay significantly higher wages for foreign workers than under current law (and to first advertise the jobs to American workers at this higher wage before hiring a foreign worker—only if the employer has 15% of their workforce paid under $60,000.)

(3) Provide spouses of foreign guest workers with work authorization.

(4) Establish a 60-day transition period for foreign workers to change jobs.

(5) Provide dual intent visas for all international students on bachelor's degree programs or above.

(6) Crack down on abusers of the work visa system by requiring employers dependant on foreign workers to pay significantly higher wages and fees than normal users of the program.

(7) Crack down on the use of the H1-B and L visas to outsource American jobs by prohibiting companies whose U.S. workforce largely consists of foreign guest workers from obtaining additional H1-B and L visas.

(8) Transparency of job openings filled by H1-B visa holders. The Secretary of Labor must establish a searchable website for posting H1-B positions, including salary and contact info for American applicants 30 days prior to requesting an H1-B visa.

(9) Bar employers from recruiting or giving preference to H1-B or OPT workers over American workers.

(10) Establish significant new authorities and penalties to prevent, detect, and deter fraud and abuse of the H1-B and L-1 visa systems by fraudulent employers.

H-4 visa holders – Right to participate in the labor economy

Married spouses of the H1 visa holders, on H-4 visas, and a majority of them being women, are consigned to being unemployed once they move to the U.S. In their home countries they were often high-earning, largely independent workers. But after moving to the U.S., they are unable to work or even open an individual bank account. They are ineligible to get a social security number and find it prohibitively difficult to get a driver's license. Their rights have been compared with those of women living in some of the most oppressive parts of the world. Some H-4 holders battle depression, and support groups have been set up to encourage people that live in what has been dubbed the "golden cage." Often, whole families relocate back to their home countries for this reason. As a result, the U.S. economy loses not just one, but the potential of two capable workers.

Even though the modern day guest worker program began in 1991, it is surprising that America – the champion of gender equality around the world – has for so long restricted so many talented women from becoming financially and, in some cases, physically independent. Women who cannot drive are often at the mercy of their husband's schedules to leave the house. And their numbers run into hundreds of thousands, making this a human rights issue.

America's competitiveness is at stake with a broken system

If current H-4 visa holders have the skills and qualifications, why should they not be able to compete on equal footing same as other job candidates? American law commits to banning discrimination by race, religion or gender, but how has this particular type of discrimination continued for so long?

In a global economy, the talent pool now operates on a global scale. No longer could the U.S. remain confined to a narrow, navel-gazing focus when competing nations believe in hiring the best, regardless of their passport.

There is high demand for specialized IT skills all over the nation, unfortunately finding candidates to fill these positions is challenging, in part because of the current immigration system. While corporate America continues to seek foreign talent justifies the acute shortage of IT professionals, the reform proposal to allow H-4 visa holders, a Right to a job will not jeopardize American jobs. Rather it will help alleviate the severe skill shortages faced in sectors like technology.

Currently, for American businesses to compete in a global technology market, there are three options:

1) Grow their own tech talent. However, the percentage of STEM (Science, Technology, Engineering and Mathematics) graduates has fallen short compared with other countries such as India and China.

2) Import talent. This is a remarkably difficult under current the immigration laws.

3) Outsource domestic work overseas, and let other countries benefit by developing talent. There is already a growing prevalence of outsourcing technology jobs.

A relaxed immigration with an increase in H-1B visas will be like a shot of adrenaline to the America economy, because it will help increase Americas revenues as the additional workers will generate tax revenues which are sorely needed.

Losing high-caliber executives and entrepreneurs

Many of America's greatest modern achievements have been built by immigrant disruptors. The U.S. is losing out on thousands, if not more, of talented people if it does not fix the current immigration system. The problem persists when companies look to hire exceptionally qualified C-level executives. If a spouse is unable to work, it is usually a non-starter in discussions when hiring top talent from abroad. Many U.S. companies have missed opportunities to hire distinctive highly-skilled talent when the spouse could not work.

As America fights to stay competitive in a global economy, it would be remiss to push out a talent pool that already exists in its own backyards. The American dream should be available for all to achieve.

Stifling this important reform is an economic issue. But more significantly, it's a human rights issue. What right, many would argue, does America have to speak out about the treatment of women in other countries when in some regards women in Saudi Arabia have greater rights than H-4 visa holders in America?

Selective Exclusion

In May 2014, the Obama Administration announced new steps to make it easier for highly skilled workers and talented researchers from other countries to contribute to the economy and ultimately become Americans. These measures reflect the commitment to attract and retain highly-skilled immigrants, towards continued economic recovery, and encouraging job creation. The new federal reform proposes allowing spouses of highly-skilled immigrant workers (H1-B visa holders) the right to work. The law will overturn the largely oppressive treatment spouses on the H-4 visa category face. The reform will affect close to 100,000 people who can finally get back to applying for jobs after months, if not years, of having to sit out of the workforce.

Specifically, the Department of Homeland Security (DHS) published a proposed rule that would—for the first time—allow work authorization for the spouses of H-1B workers who have begun the process of applying for a green card through their employers. Once enacted, this proposed rule would empower these spouses to put their own education and skills to work for the country that they and their families now call home. This rule change was requested in a "We the People" petition to the White House and an Executive Order to that effect will put this proposal into a federal law.

Under existing regulations, Department Of Homeland Security does not extend employment authorization to dependents (also known as H-4 non immigrants) of H-1B nonimmigrant workers. The change proposed by DHS, would allow H-4 dependent spouses of certain H-1B nonimmigrant workers to request employment authorization, as long as the H-1B worker has already started the process of seeking lawful permanent residence through employment.

Eligible individuals would include H-4 dependent spouses of principal H-1B workers in any of the two conditions:

1) Employment Authorization Document will be granted to the spouses of those H1-B workers whose I 140 is cleared. It is a stage in the Green Card processing that has a severe backlog of many years.

   OR

2) Employment Authorization Document will be granted to the spouses of those H1-B workers whose 6 years have been completed. You can stay in the United Sates after the maxing out of your H1-B visa, only if your Green Card processing has been started.

Encouraging as this may seem, this may not cater to the woes of the H-4 visa community in its entirety. The reform proposal is focused at only those individuals that have a Green Card petition filed on their behalf by their spouses employers., and these numbers are small as compared to the overall population of H-4 visa holders already present inside the country. In the year 2013 alone, the US government has issued 96,753 H-4 visas to married spouses of H-1B visa holders.

It would greatly help to consider that the real beneficiaries of employment authorization would also be those H-4 visa holders whose spouses are subjugated and abused by their visa sponsoring employers, and those that consistently face un employment and visa shunting.

10 BACK TO THE FUTURE

The quaint suburb of Nerul in Navi Mumbai, where I lived has a total population of approximately 200,000 residents and is surrounded by seven colleges offering professional degree courses. Students from far distance arrive here with a dream to build not just their careers, but a future that they envision. And these young visionaries are the youngsters that dream of being future engineers, doctors, media professionals, architects.

But I must confess, I have been fortunate, to be associating with these kids housed in apartments and hostels around me. I may sound a bit cruel, but yes, it is a pleasure to watch them struggle with their day to day college chores, because despite these chores, their eyes twinkle with a dream. The dreams these kids dream, is not endowed upon them, by virtue of their parents, but are dreams that these youngsters have earned somewhere in their journey of the hardships of their college life. I often confront them, and often I end up being questioned; often I am challenged with their sentiments. But the debate with my young friends continues to question me. And these kids are smart, as you will see -

The debate we have is over globalization and the migrant workforce, a subject that has become global. It is a well established fact that companies in industrial economies have become dependent on the work of migrants. It is also a known fact that migrants form a sub-class of people working in jobs with the lowest wages, least security and most dangerous conditions. While on one hand, nations seek to end the spontaneous movement of less skilled workers. On the other, they seek to channel migration into programs that would deliver Indian migrants to the corporate industry as a contracted workforce. This duality is not unique to those that have traveled, but to these youngsters, it still is a matter of confusion.

Many of my young friends express their desire to serve in the domestic labor market, but seek gratification to their efforts. Simply put, they question me – why despite my hardships, am I still sought by the big organizations – only to be labeled as a 'coolie worker'? Why do I have to sign a bond if I am in demand and paid the highest when no one else can?

As I try my best to explain that the ideas and practice of social inequality, of inclusion and exclusion, are very old and that these take centre stage even in today's wage discrimination debate. As I try and explain that these ideas became codified in the "legal" justification for the injustices, and that today inequality is being re-created and reproduced as a need by a global economic system.

Yet comes another question, and this one's interesting – "Why then should our workers complain if they are f**ked overseas, when our own Indian company treats us as s**t"? I bet our minister's must own stake in these big companies. "

How am I to answer this?

Ever since the 1990s, when developing economies began competing in world markets, a global labor market has started taking shape. More than a billion people today have entered the labor force. A massive "farm to factory" movement has sharply accelerated the growth of productivity and has increased the per capita incomes of China and India, bringing hundreds of millions of people out of poverty.

While the developed economies have been productive by investing in labor-saving technologies and tapping the low-cost labor outside of their nation's borders, today however, the strains on the labor market are becoming increasingly apparent.

In these developed economies, the demand for high-skill labor is now growing faster than ever before, but the demand for low-skill labor seems to be very low. Based on current trends in population, education, and labor demand, the Mckinsey labor report released in June 2012 projects that by the year 2020, the global economy could face the following hurdles:

- Have a shortfall of 38 - 40 million workers with college or postgraduate degrees,
- Have a shortfall of 45 million workers with secondary education in developing economies,
- Have an oversupply of 90-95 million low-skill workers (those without college training in advanced economies or those without even secondary education in developing economies)

Already, in the developed economies, there is an alarming income polarization, with evident income inequality as the lower-skill workers (75 million) experience unemployment, under employment, and stagnating wages and are competing with high skilled workers from abroad at lower costs.

As the global labor force approaches 3.5 billion in 2030, these trends are now gathering force and spreading to other developing economies such as China and India as well.

But for China, however, the dynamics of the aging population makes the labor challenges even more difficult, reducing their participation in the global labor supply chain. The aging population is estimated to be close to 360 million older people who will no longer be working. Add to this, the 38 million college-educated workers, whose skills will already be in short supply.

The world is graying at a break-neck pace and that's bad news for the global economy. By 2020, 13 countries will be "super-aged" -- with more than 20% of the population over 65 -- according to a report on *Global aging* by Moody's Investor Service. That number will rise to 34 nations by 2030. Only three qualify now: Germany, Italy and Japan.

The unprecedented pace of aging will have a significant negative effect on economic growth over the next two decades across all regions.

Greece and Finland will turn "super-aged" by 2015. Eight countries, including France and Sweden, will have joined them by 2020.Canada, Spain and the U.K. will be "super-aged" by 2025, and the U.S. will follow by 2030. And the problem isn't confined to Europe and North America. Singapore and Korea will be in that category by 2030, while China will also face "severe aging pressures."

Aging populations create problems because there could be fewer working people to drive economic growth and support the retired population.

Unfortunately, in the U.S. for instance, studies are showing that except for upper- and top-level management, for semi-skilled and skilled positions most companies don't want workers with more than 15 - 20 years of experience.

People in their mid-40's with relevant college degrees with 20 plus years of relevant work experience are often reporting that no company will interview them for a job in their field (especially if they have been laid off or their previous employer went out of business.)

And as for the idea of going back to school for a semester or two and picking up "new job skills", most employers don't want beginners with decades of unrelated work experience. Young folks have the illusion that if they work hard and show dedication they'll advance. Older folks (even under 50) know that in most cases that's not true. And they know employers are not going to "groom" them for a long-term career when they're already in their mid-40's or older.

Therefore, a majority of the supply to the global labor force will come from India - with 50 % of its population under the age of 25 and more than 65% below the age of 35. India churns out most science and engineering graduates every year to the current global labor market demand bringing a competitive advantage.

As people migration across borders will accelerate, job displacement and the need to fill open local job positions from abroad will become even more evident. Businesses operating in this skills-scarce world will need to know how to find talent pools with the skills they need and build strategies for hiring, retaining, and training the workers who will give them the continued competitive advantage.

Recently, India has been inducted into the Washington Accord, and has become one of the 17 countries that share professional qualifications of its youth. India became a permanent member of the Washington Accord, which would enable global recognition of Indian degrees and increase the mobility of engineers to the USA and other countries for jobs. International mobility of engineering graduates from Indian Institutes of Technology (IITs) has not been an issue given the global recognition of these institutes, but this has not been the case with the graduates from the 1,300-odd other engineering colleges in India. By becoming a permanent member of the Washington Accord, Indian engineering graduates will be considered to have met the academic requirements necessary to take up the practice of engineering in any of the signatory countries. The Washington Accord aims to promote mobility and quality assurance across countries. Besides recognition for Indian engineering degrees, membership of the international accreditation agreement will ensure a minimum global quality for all engineering institutions in India.

Recruitment of fresh engineering graduates by foreign employers will therefore accelerate. Paying low to its workers and bidding them high to foreign clients too will spin a new business paradigm for businesses dependent on pushing Indian labor across borders.

As knowledge becomes the new power, workers pushed across borders by broker agents and those being cheated of their pay or those stranded abroad will see a huge increase. So while, developed economies will increase their dependence on foreign workers, the growing social inequality amongst the worker classes will drastically increase their social costs as well.

Indian economy has undergone important structural change shifting from agriculture to services and industrial sectors. This has happened due to the processes of opening up the economy through globalization, privatization and modernization. Therefore, the movement from agricultural-led growth to industry and services demands technological up gradation, acquiring different sets of skills, and knowledge. There is evidence to suggest that human capital of India's labor force is not geared enough to be competent in the global economy.

India is once again on the cusp of economic growth. The rapid financial reforms by opening up the Indian markets to foreign investments will continue to aid in the creation of tremendous employment opportunities for the workers in the informal sector as well.

Already, India's talent shortages are hitting the bottom line of business and are reflected in the increase in attrition rates of skilled manpower and wage inflation in various business verticals. This situation is compounded by the increase in demand for skilled and semi – skilled manpower in various sectors within India alone.

India produces over 350,000 engineering graduates annually, and only about one fifth are able to satisfy the skill expectations of firms and enterprises in various sectors to find immediate employment. Another two fifth settle for jobs whose profile is far below the level of skills connoted by their degrees. The remaining settle for the employment that is unrelated to their graduate training. Thus unemployment among the youth is a serious issue which needs immediate concern.

This issue is also connected with the nature of education system and how appropriate this education system is to generate an employable work force. Universities and educational institutions supply enough to meet the demands of the industry but lack in experienced people, which in turn creates, an imbalance. This imbalance is critical to the growth of the specific sector; however the focus needs to be not only on creating employment rather should be focusing on employability.

Employability is the capacity of an individual to get an employment and hold on to an employment. It is the capability of the individual to move in the labor market and realize his/her potential to earn a livelihood through sustained employment. It depends on the knowledge, skills and the attitudes that the individuals possess and the way he/she use the skills and present them to an employer. From the point of view of the individual, employability skills are the career capital that a worker needs to get a job and acquire job specific skills, while on the job.

India has a stock of some 22 million graduates, including 6 million science graduates, 1.2 million with engineering degrees and 600,000 doctors. India's higher education system contributes about 350,000 engineers and 2.5 million university graduates annually to our workforce. India has more than 15,000 colleges and just fewer than 10 million students. But Secondary School Students those in Grade 8th thru 12th count as approximately 1 billion students. While workers needs are addressed, those of the aspiring workers (students) needs are often overlooked. But even though the numbers are large, employability and not unemployment lies at the core of the issues.

The Academia-Industry Mismatch

Because the rapid globalization creates jobs in certain market sectors and job losses in other market sectors, students entering in the job market have a compelling time in finding employment. Students often find that the classroom teaching is inadequate in helping them source employment or even once they are in a job, remain employable. Companies too spend a considerable amount of time and resources in training them on-the-job.

Though this mismatch is less prevailing in educational institutions closer to the cities, it brings emphasis to the visiting companies' on-campus for recruitment. Needlessly, the higher the salary offered by the recruitment on-campus, leads to the educational institution being famous and charging a heavy admission fee for the prospective students. Corruption underlies this vicious circle where educational institutions charge premium fees in exchange for employment placement with a high paying employer. While employers give preferential value for students belonging to a certain institution, they offer an employment bond in exchange for recruitment.

Educational Institutions globally have a constant need for companies to recruit their fresh graduates via on-campus recruitment drives. Employers therefore become a brand value proposition to these colleges, dictating terms of recruitment. Colleges in turn, disconnected from the corporate needs, are unable to effectively train their students. The concern faced by many colleges today is that they are disconnected from industry and lack effective recruitment efforts. The growing alumni network - those graduated from previous years are ineffective in recommending existing students to their employers, and hence have an ineffective social viral growth.

Because bigger employers are seen as better employers, employers coming to recruit on campus are often seen as a brand value by the educational institutions and thus are dependent on referring certain employers. Because of this, On-campus recruitment drives often exclude start up firms with entrepreneurial opportunities. There is therefore an urgent need for effective technological innovative techniques to drive recruitment efforts and make accessible more employment opportunities to graduating students.

Students enrolled in professional courses often complain of the lack of hands-on live projects to work on, as mandated by their course work. The academia - corporate mismatch and the lack of hands-on training often limits possibilities of fresher's getting on-campus recruitment necessary for their first job. Students commit document fraud towards recruitment often fudging experience letters and project work. Fraudulent project reports are submitted by students, and purchased at various retail outlets to fulfill this critical requirement.

In lieu of the campus recruitment drives, it was found from the student's viewpoint that often the classroom learning experience did not match with the expectations from the employers. The On campus recruitment was reserved to the high prolific companies, which was not necessarily in the best interest of the students. The procedures were exhaustive making recruitment for fresher grads more difficult. Employers, scrutinize every applicant during a campus interview with an eagle eye. The recruitment procedure was exhaustive thus making recruitment for fresher grads even more difficult. To offset the costs of recruitment and training of a fresher employee, employers demand a legal bond from them thus creating a bonded / contractual labor workforce. On campus recruitment therefore has increased the labor contracts.

It is important for the students to know what is expected from the corporate world and their efforts to being able to fit in. Accessing live hands-on projects as part of the course work, building a corporate-student relationship to enable them a job offer early & prior to graduation, and being imbibed in the community framework of working professionals and recruiters, via the alumni network is inadequate. In the final year of their graduation, students most

- Whether the rate of pay is expressed on an annual, monthly, weekly, biweekly or hourly basis,
- A Statement of the expected hours per week that job will require,
- The date on which the job is expected to begin,
- The date on which the job is expected to end,
- The number of persons expected to be employed for the job along with the following –
- The job title,
- The job description,
- The city and state of the physical location at which the work will be performed,
- Description of the process by which a United States worker may submit an application to be considered for the job,

[Accountability] Conditions for employers – Employers will not advertise any jobs stating are available for persons who are, or who may, become H1-B visa holders nor will give priority / preference to them,

1. The employer shall not place, outsource, lease or otherwise contract for the placement of an H1-B visa holder to another employer,

[Worker Protection] Information provided to the H1-B Visa holder upon issuance of visa –

1. It will be the Obligation of the Department of Labor to inform the rights to the H1-B visa holder
2. The visa issuing officer shall provide –
    - A brochure outlining the employer's obligations and the employee's rights under the federal law, including labor and wage protections,
    - Contact information for federal agencies that can offer more information or assistance in clarifying employer's obligations and worker's rights

[Governance] L-1 Visa fraud and abuse protections - If the beneficiary of a petition is coming to the United States to open or be employed in a new facility, the petition may be approved for only 12 months only if the employer operating the new facility has –

1. A business plan,
2. Sufficient physical premises to carry out the proposed business activities,
3. The financial ability to commence doing business immediately upon the approval of the petition,
4. The Secretary of Homeland Security shall work cooperatively with the Secretary of State to verify a company or facility's existence in the United States and abroad,
5. The Secretary of Homeland Security may not permit the use of blanket petitions to import foreign workers,
6. The employer shall not place, outsource, lease or otherwise contract for the placement of an L-1 visa holder to another employer,

I observed that due to the volume of reported employer violations, there has been an ever-growing awareness to the 'foreign and migrant worker' issue globally. Host nations have been re-structuring their immigration policies to accommodate the growing demands of cross-border movement of individuals, those competing directly with the local workforce's right to a job. In terms of maintaining accessibility of both classes of workers the path to employment, it is a delicate balance.

While streamlining the recruitment process is a top agenda in their respective countries, the burden therefore is on the individual workers. The 'Good faith' in hiring of foreign talent that guarantees non replacement of the domestic labor pool is slowly getting restored.

As every country is governed by the rule of its land, the immigration border policies of these host nations are getting stringent allowing only the best and the brightest into the country. While legislation is a hot bed of debate, very often, changes to the policies that govern the movement of skilled labor from overseas, have been a long and an enduring task.

As nations streamline their policies to bring accountability of its employers, an Open Registry of Background screened and Verified Workers initiative will aim to equip Indian knowledge workers that are sought in earnest by employers globally.

As part of the documentary proof involved in the filing of a work visa petition on behalf of a prospective citizen from abroad, often requests are made to determine credential equivalency checks as a measure to evaluate the workers compatibility against the established domestic standards. These documents are often submitted without a guarantee of been 'verified and authenticated'. As a result, today there are an alarmingly increasing numbers of citizens from abroad who are newly termed as 'visa orphans', deemed out-of-status by virtue of the document manipulation.

The Open Registry will offer the flexibility in the global labor market thereby minimizing the brokerage of Intellectual capital, and the related subjugation of human resource from India. The main objective of the Open Registry therefore is to - "Promote India: Qualify the Source, and Own the TARP" –

1. Transparency: - Reduce the time to market in making the hiring decisions that will expedite immigration processing
2. Accountability - Remove background verification redundancy, and initiate a best practice initiative.
3. Reliability - Focus on the best & brightest talent thereby increasing the competitive edge, higher salaries.
4. Professionalism - Foster circular migration against merely managing the flow of migration, enabling continuous employment for workers

Real Jobs, Real People: Match the Best & Brightest - The Open Registry shall serve as the largest open source registry of background screened and verified knowledge workers which are accessible online. Bringing knowledge workers and the company they work for or aspire to work with, on one common platform of authentication. The value proposition aims to:

1. Foster circular migration against merely managing it.
2. Reduce the time to market in making the hiring decisions
3. Creation of a permanent and unique member profile page on an industry-wide reference database that is circulated across the web
4. Enhanced credibility of registered and verified information
5. No hassles of repeat background check for every new employment, thereby speeding up joining formalities.
6. Transparent Background Verification Process
7. Deterrent for competing job applicants with inflated and faked profiles
8. Expedite immigration processing
9. Remove background verification redundancy
10. Focus on the best & brightest talent
11. Initiate a best practice initiative by making the jobseeker / student to adopt a model, based on Transparency, Accountability, and Reliability
12. Increased demand will rise the competitive edge thereby giving guest workers from India the prevailing wage at par with the local work force while working overseas
13. Enable immigration attorneys from host nations to seek qualified workers online in real time on behalf of their employers
14. Enable existing visa orphans, an opportunity to get back in visa status thus re aligning to their socio-economic value proposition in their current country of residence
15. Give control to the individual job seeker, minimizing their dependency on the recruiting agents

The Open Registry will hope to achieve the following in the Indian recruitment industry

1. Protect the interest of its members and help them establish, promote and sustain opportunities in the global labor recruitment process, which in turn would create an ecosystem of experienced, qualified, and sincere resource pool of talented knowledge workers.
2. Promote knowledge workers whose origin is India and help employers achieve enhanced productivity aiding sourcing of most skilled human resource targets.

3. Promote, protect and develop the Intellectual Property of the knowledge workers of India.
4. Educate knowledge workers and their employers about the laws, regulations, best practices, and thereby mobilizing them in a direction to transform this sector to a growth and prosperity
5. Provide a common platform for all the stakeholders viz., the knowledge workers, governmental agencies, regulatory bodies, policymakers, the Law Enforcement Authorities, the Regulators, educational institutions, and career portals
6. Facilitate the creation of employment opportunities
7. Make India's skilled workforce immediately accessible to the global employers
8. Create an ecosystem of mentors and workers that are reliable and knowledgeable

The repository, in my opinion, may bind most of the grey areas in the global labor recruitment industry. The Open Registry then may help connect and address the additional growing areas of concern; in the pre departure, employment and capacity building processes/phases as well as address a few recession-specific concerns that affect Indian workers. A few of these concerns are –

In the pre departure phase:

- Lack of adequate regulatory mechanism to check worker's exploitation - There is no mechanism to check whether an individual worker is exploited by the overseas employer even when exploitation is reported to the Indian government by the workers.
- Lack of awareness among migrants of their employers, recruiting agents, emigration rules applicable, etc - There is evidence of mal-practices and exploitation by recruiting agents both in the source as well as the destination countries however workers have limited knowledge of their rights when affected by malpractice.
- Slowdown in the employment sectors abroad on account of the economic crisis- Even though some sectors shrink employment opportunities, there is little or no awareness to the same by the prospective job seeker in India. Often, lured by agents, workers end up paying money for jobs that do not exist.

In the employment phase:

- Indians are perceived as being less productive as compared to workers in other low cost countries such as the Philippines- Lack of sector specific skills and training helpful in gaining employment overseas alienates workers that learn skills on the job, and are perceived less productive
- Ineffective regulations in destination countries leading to overstay of migrants- Exploitation and torture by the employers by holding passports, non-payment of salaries, etc and the lack of awareness to visa laws and rule of the land often leads to workers overstaying beyond the expiry of their visas. Often employers in the destination countries evade high administered fees to hire legal foreign workers and resort to illegal migration resulting in unfavorable working and living conditions
- Ineffective trade unions that aim to protect the rights of migrants - Discouragements to trade unions that protect the rights of migrants arise mostly due to the fact that a worker is seen as a commodity with a focus on inward remittances only. Aspects of human rights violations are completely ignored and unions receive no support from the government.

In the Capacity building phase:- There is a serious lack of mechanism to identify potential destination countries and its sectors for employment because of which there is little or no skill developmental courses or any adequate institutionalized training. There is a serious limitation to understand the dynamism in the training curriculum to suit with the foreign labor market needs

Recession specific concerns: - Because there is a significant reduction in overseas employment in sectors affected by economic crisis, there are more stringent immigration rules that lead to an increase in the exploitation of migrant labor and racism. Due to which there is an alarming increase in illegal migrants, as laid off workers do not return home and the growing number of 'visa orphans' of Indian origin in foreign countries is a major concern. Recession specific factors also include a significant reduction in migrant earnings due to reduced overtime opportunities with an increase in the number of working hours. Recession induced financial burden of loans on the migrants and the lack of assistance on return to home country related to employment, financial and social assistance from Indian government is non-existent

Important considerations and need for immediate action required is:-

- Rigorous inspection of the background of both the employer and migrant worker;
- An open registry of workers whose background checks and overseas employment history has been verified be set up to expedite futuristic employment opportunities overseas;
- Online migrant tracking mechanism may be introduced to track the migrants from the date of departure to the date of arrival and permanent residency in other country;
- Setting up of a help-desk to help and provide information to the migrant. This may make the migrant aware of the lay-offs and difficulties caused by the financial crisis;
- Visa Facilitation Services (VFS), must make available to prospective visa applicants and provide printed hand-outs regarding information for workers their rights and make available information to seek assistance while serving abroad. This information must be current and updated specific to the visiting country;
- Development of comprehensive web portal for migration related information dissemination;
- In Indian embassies, a separate cell may be created to constantly interact with the key employers of Indian migrants to understand their plan for both retrenching and recruiting Indian migrants;
- Indian embassies may collaborate with various local media to popularize facilities available for migrant Indian workers;
- An extension counter of employment may be opened in all major airports, wherein returnee jobless workers could register providing all the relevant information of his/her past experience and future preferences;
- An 'Overseas Worker Counseling' counter may be opened in the major airports to assist and guide the employment opportunities in India for the returnees. These could be created in partnership with organizations with corporate social responsibility participation;

- An emergency employment scheme may be introduced to take care of the returnees with a safety net of unemployment allowance;
- Undertake awareness campaign for the available skill up gradation programmes;

Long-term actions required:-

- Psychometric Tests - Introduction of psychometric test for the migrants to ensure the best match of individuals occupation and working environment and make recommendations based on test results;
- A Review system - Enforce stringent measures to regulate recruitment agents and receive feedback from the placed migrants and migrant families may be sought and analyzed to renew the registration of the recruitment agencies;
- Forge Partnerships – Focus on building and strengthening partnerships with border agencies of host nations to implement stringent measures to combat illegal migration;
- Pre-departure Orientation - A mandatory country specific pre-departure orientation course may be introduced for all migrants;
- A Welfare fund - A contributory welfare fund may be created for the benefit of migrants against job losses or any other requirements needing mobility and repatriation;
- Job fairs may be organized in foreign countries.
- Mobility partnership agreements may be signed with clear stipulations on terms of employment, working and living conditions, rights and responsibilities of the Indian migrant workers.
- Periodic consultation between the home and host country governments
- Government should develop a framework to identify countries and industries which have good employment potential, such as, hospitality, travel & tourism, healthcare etc. Once identified, government should formulate adequate capacity building programs for these industries and impart training programs via effective government - university linkages;

- Foreign employers may be encouraged to set up training institutions in India to provide training before departure;

It is estimated that over a 100 million people will migrate between 2005 and 2050. Developing countries will supply manpower to numerous aging populations to meet skill shortages that are already showing. That will mean large-scale migration across continents. As knowledge becomes the new power in this globalised world, movement of both skilled and unskilled labor is inevitable to allow processes to deliver to global demands. Globalization has also resulted in job losses making migration to other countries a reality as desperate people try to make good their job losses and look for new opportunities.

Foreign Direct Investment by foreign nations in India, especially in the manufacturing sector will create tremendous employment opportunities – both for the local as well as citizens from abroad. People movement will see a steady rise and continue to accelerate. The issues related to human migration therefore will be a top priority as that will increase the social costs of nations dependant on foreign labor.

12 FINAL WORD

International labor migration is defined as the movement of people from one country to another for the purpose of employment. With an estimated 105 million people working in a country other than their country of birth, today labor mobility has become a key feature of globalization. In the global economy, migrant workers earned US$ 440 billion in the year 2011 alone, and the World Bank estimates that more than $350 billion of that total was transferred to developing countries in the form of remittances. However, despite the efforts made to ensure the protection of migrant workers, many remain vulnerable and assume significant risks during the migration process.

Even when properly managed, labor migration has far-reaching potential for the migrants, their communities, the countries of origin and destination, and for employers. While job creation in the home country is the core objective, demographic, social and economic factors are what drives migration. As a result of which, a growing number of both sending and receiving countries view international labor migration as an integral part of their national development and employment strategies.

While on one hand, countries of origin benefit from labor migration because it relieves unemployment pressures and contributes to development through remittances, knowledge transfer, and the creation of business and trade networks. On the other hand, for destination countries facing labor shortages, orderly and well-managed labor migration can lighten the labor scarcity and facilitate mobility.

Migration Trends in North America and Europe

North America is traditionally a destination for migration flows, a big part of which comes from Mesoamerica, but mainly from Mexico. While very different from each other, Mesoamerica and the Caribbean are considered mainly the regions of origin and transit.

The available data reflect a small recovery in the growth of Mesoamerican migration flows to the northern countries of the region (Canada and the United States of America) in 2012.

While it is still unclear on the size of Mesoamerican migration flows that may be observed in the next few years in the United States, some analysis have shown that the net migration flows from Mesoamerica to the United States over at least the next decade are likely to increase, but are very unlikely to reach the levels found in the 1990s (around 600,000 annually). Possibly the available data suggest that the net inflows will be around 400,000 per year.

Regarding the Caribbean, migration inflows are mostly from East Asia, Africa and South America, while people movement out of the Caribbean are usually towards North America and the United Kingdom. Although the Caribbean Community has a scheme to facilitate the free movement of people, this applies to only certain categories of migrants.

Additionally, the Americas, generally speaking are vulnerable to natural disasters. Particularly, the Caribbean, which has the least capacity to deal with the numerous challenges arising from these catastrophes. This mix of vulnerability and reduced capacities will foresee ably have implications for human mobility in the region as it has been the case in the past, especially in Haiti.

The consolidation of new locations that attract migratory flows, such as Belize, El Salvador, Mexico, Panama, and Trinidad and Tobago, is a developing trend. This phenomenon is rooted in different factors, such as the setting of new economic activities demanding low-skilled workforce, high economic growth sustained for long periods of time, the process of dollarization in the economies of some countries, and high levels of outward migration in certain locations, which have caused a shortage of domestic labor force replaced by workers from neighboring countries. Job displacement seems to be at the core of such migration. However, most of the migration is irregular.

There has also been a significant growth in the intraregional flows from developed countries to developing countries, which is a growing trend. The people migration is mainly composed of retirees and pensioners. Although their aggregate number might not be significant, the growth rate is substantial and its economic effect is appreciable in certain locations.

Extra-continental migration flows originating from developing Asian and African countries have grown meaningfully in the United States, mostly during the past 10 years. Reports suggest that the number of arrests of irregular migrants from Asian and African countries has increased significantly from 2000 to date. Bangladesh, China, Eritrea, India, Nigeria, the Republic of Korea and South Africa are the countries of origin of the majority of the migratory in flows.

Migration management is an increasingly critical component of security policies in the region as transnational organized criminal networks are increasingly involved in migrant smuggling, human trafficking, and identity and travel document falsification and alteration. Abuses and crimes committed against migrants, especially against migrants in transit, are growing significantly.

The number of returnees has significantly increased in the region. Stricter deportation policies as well as economic crises in developed receiving states are the main causes of these returns. Some of the communities of major returning people are reporting to be experiencing difficulties to reintegrate returnees and of providing them with services like health and education.

Unaccompanied children migrating to the United States is a growing trend as well. The most important drivers of this trend are family reunification and labor opportunities.

As per the International Migration Office (IMO), the latest estimated migrant population in South-Eastern Europe, Eastern Europe and

Central Asia is 29.9 million. Although this figure has decreased since 1990, the share of immigrant population here is at 8.4 per cent, which is significantly higher than the world's average of 3.1 per cent. At the same time, the region continues to be primarily characterized by emigration processes, with emigrant population holding an average share of 16.7 per cent of the total population, when the world's average is 2.9%.

Population relocations happen primarily within the boundaries of the region. And around 90 per cent of the 24.6 million of international migrants from within the Eastern Europe and Central Asia moved internally within this sub region. Female migrants continued to present a majority within the total migrants in South-Eastern Europe, Eastern Europe and Central Asia, and has gradually grown from 55.9 per cent to 56.6 per cent.

One of the primary reasons for migration in the South-Eastern Europe, Eastern Europe and Central Asia remains the search for employment opportunities. Foreign migrant workers from Central Asia and Eastern Europe continue to seek employment in the labor markets of more economically developed neighbors, such as the Russian Federation, Kazakhstan, and also Azerbaijan, in the construction, service and oil-producing industries.

The strong tourism industry of Montenegro and Turkey attracts temporary migrant workers from within and outside the region as well. Additionally, a fair amount of labor migration, especially from Eastern Europe and South-Eastern Europe, are directed towards the European Union.

At the same time, while in the past only a handful of industrialized countries were identified as countries of destination, today the patterns of movement are such that most countries in the region are simultaneously, countries of origin, transit and destination. Primarily, the desire to obtain temporary employment in the neighboring countries draws the attention of migrant workers to the non-traditional immigration countries. For example, citizens of Uzbekistan do not only choose the Russian Federation or Kazakhstan as employment destinations but also come to work in the border regions of Kyrgyzstan and Tajikistan.

However, to some extent, multidirectional migratory patterns also apply to longer-term migrants who decide to settle in the countries in the South-Eastern Europe, Eastern Europe and Central Asia region primarily for family reasons, and also as students or inter-corporate transferees.

Mode 4 and the UN Convention on the Rights Of Migrants

David Bacon, in his book "Illegal People – How Globalization Creates Migration and Criminalizes Immigrants" has succinctly detailed the functioning of the global labor policy at the WTO. He says that – "There is a political alliance between countries that export labor and the corporations who dominate the World Trade Organization. Many countries that send their workers to the developed world depend on the remittances to finance their social services, provide capital to their small scale industries, all the while keeping a lid on the social discontent over poverty and joblessness. And corporations that use such displaced labor have a growing interest with the governments that help regulate the system that supplies such labor to them."

Worldwide the flow of people movement is caused by displacement which is generally self initiated. Simply put, people move at their own free will and discretion, trying to find economic opportunities and to reunite with their families. In the process, creating new communities in the countries that they now call home. And these communities are not only the unskilled people, but the skilled workers as well. There are a significant new group of nations, where the average citizen is poor, but the nation as a whole is technologically advanced and economically powerful - like China, India, Brazil, Russia and Thailand. Technical education in these countries is both cheap and advanced, thanks to the internet and the easy movement of ethnic technocrats between the developed world and their countries of origin.

Trade policies and policies related to people movement are often debated separately. However, the idea of managing the people moving between countries is growing in nations participating in the global economy. At the WTO Hong Kong Summit in 2005, a proposal was introduced for the first time to begin channeling the movement of people along with the movement of capital and goods. As the WTO further regulated the modes in which services are provided in the world economy, it began by proposing the management of people movement by considering them as being the "providers of services" in what is called as the 'Mode 4'.

The Mode 4 program by the United Nations was originally proposed for skilled workers and executives, including sales people, corporate managers and specialists, foreign employees of corporate subsidiaries and independent contractors like doctors and architects. While labor exporting the countries like India and China have been advocating to expand the range of jobs to include construction workers, domestic workers and other less skilled workers as well.

Under the Mode 4, that defines the people movement Internationally, it also sets the criteria for the guest worker programs. As in all guest worker programs, the visas of the workers would require them to remain employed, and they would be deported if they lost their jobs. Contractors would be allowed to recruit workers in one country and sell their labor in another. The visas of these workers would be temporary and they would not be able to become permanent residents. Countries contracting for these guest workers could regulate the number admitted and establish conditions under which they would be employed. Countries would assign a annual quota to the import of foreign workers.

Even though the people movement is governed by the WTO and the participating countries, the WTO does not establish the minimum wages and conditions / standards of employment, rather they are regulated by the UN's International Labor Organization instead. Over many decades, however, the ILO has been unable to create any mandatory standards or wages, nor has put in place any enforceable mechanism to punish any countries or their corporations that violate their voluntary standards.

Because of the economic reforms, communities are displaced due to privatization and ending of subsidies. These are all mandated by the WTO and the International Trade Agreements. Displacement will continue under this scheme while protection for workers and migrants will be voluntary and ineffective. On the contrary, it will produce migrants in a large scale and give the corporations and their governments the freedom to exploit them without regulations or limits.

Developing countries like India and China, that export their labor, however have an alternative framework for protecting the rights and status of their overseas migrant population. Instead of regulating movement of people through the WTO, countries could ratify and implement the UN International Convention on the Protection Of the Rights of All Migrant Workers and Members of Their Families.

This UN International Convention was adopted in 1990 – same year the American guest worker program, the H-1B program began!

Under the UN Convention, basic human rights of all migrant workers and their families, documented or undocumented is considered. The convention supports family reunification, establishes the principle of equal employment opportunity with the citizens of the host country in terms of employment and education, protection against collective deportation and makes both the sending and receiving countries responsible for protecting these rights.

All countries retain the right to determine who is admitted inside their territories and under what conditions are people allowed to be gainfully employed. It does not answer all answers of migration and people movement in a world economic system, however it takes two basic steps that still hinder the debate on immigration. It recognizes the new global scale of migration and its performance, and it begins by protecting the rights of its people, especially those with the lease power – migrants themselves.

In the U.S immigration debate, those supporting restrictions claim that the protections are directed only towards undocumented immigrants. But maintaining such a distinction between legal and illegal status its self has become a code for preserving inequality, a tired system dividing people into those with rights and those without. The guest worker schemes also set up similar ties – another form of illegality. Once established, the growing inequality eventually affects all – including legal or permanent residents. The effects of such a social inequality spreads beyond immigrants to citizens as well, especially in a society that has historically defined unequal status by skin color and sex.

We Work to Live, We Don't Live to Work

Citizenship is a global phenomenon and a complex issue in a world where migrant communities span borders and exist in more than one place simultaneously. The creation of transnational communities exists at different stages of development in the flow of migrants from Algeria to France, Turkey to Germany, Jamaica or Pakistan to the United Kingdom, the Philippines to South Korea and Hong Kong and from the developing to the developed countries worldwide.

Today an increasing percentage of migration is made up of indigenous migrants who share culture and language. They belong to transnational communities, retaining ties to their communities of origin in their homeland, while they establish new communities as they migrate in search of work. And indigenous migrants of such transnational communities move back and forth through these established community networks as much as they can.

However, in transnational communities preserving indigenous language and traditions is not easy. The survival of indigenous culture is at risk. The experience of racism against indigenous people and migrants of a specific community in fact enforces a search for cultural identity to strengthen the ability of communities to resist.

Also transnational communities do not exist in isolation. Residents of such communities do not see themselves simply as victims of an unfair system, but as actors that are capable of reproducing culture, of providing economic support to families in their towns of origin and of seeking social justice in the country where they have migrated to. These communities have a lot to offer to the larger world, but they need an opportunity to define their experience and to propose solutions to problems that correspond to the real problems in their lives. Transnational migrants insist that they have important social as well as political rights, both in their communities of origin as well as in their communities abroad.

A sensible immigration policy therefore would be to recognize and value the communities of the migrants and see their support as desirable. It would reinforce indigenous culture and language, rather than treating them as a threat. While at the same time, seeking to integrate immigrants into a broader community around them, giving them a voice to be heard, rather than promoting social exclusion, isolation and segregation. It would protect the rights of immigrants as part of protecting the rights of all working people.

Unfortunately, most migration in today's global economy is forced migration, as a result of dislocation. Yet, migration will continue. We move and travel because we can – it is what makes us human. Curiosity and the desire to know our fellow human beings, even on the other side of the planet, makes us who we are. We admire those who speak many languages, and those who can move swiftly from community to community, communicating with a broad variety of people.

Today the huge global movement of people has connected families and communities over thousands of miles and many borders, creating links between people that will inevitably grow. Immigration policy should make that movement possible, instead of seeing everywhere a threat. Freedom of movement is a human right. But selling foreign workers to the employers should not be the price for gaining it.

Beyond equality is solidarity

Working people have a great advantage in the global economy. They are part of a great migrant stream, creating a human bond that connects the countries of the developed and the developing world. Today working people of all countries are asked to accept continuing globalization, in which capital is free to go wherever it wants. Needlessly, migrants must also have the same freedom, with rights and status equal to those of anyone else. People in India, Mexico, Bangladesh, China and the United States, and every other country need the same things – secure jobs at a living wage, rights in their workplaces and communities and the freedom to travel and seek a future for their families.

The borders between countries should be common ground where people and their communities can come together, and must not be lines that pull them apart.

ABOUT THE AUTHOR

Rajiv Dabhadkar has over 25 years of experience in education and technology sectors. Rajiv has lived in the United States for more than a decade helping large companies deal in the movement of global talent. Rajiv has been a proponent of migration for over a decade and has actively moved forward the debate on Indo-American work visa related migration policies. He is the Founder of "The National Organization for Software and Technology Professionals" since 2004. He is the author of "American Work Permit – Official Rules & Regulations of American Work Visa". He has testified against the work visa program abuse leading to the drafting of the 'Visa Fraud and Abuse Prevention Act of 2007' aimed to prevent visa misuse and document fraud in the immigration process. His research work has been cited by the UK Border Agency as well as the US Homeland Security. Rajiv is a KaramVeer Global fellow and is a recipient of the coveted KaramVeer Chakra for Social Justice in 2014, initiated by the United Nations.

www.ingramcontent.com/pod-product-compliance
Lightning Source LLC
Chambersburg PA
CBHW071424170526
45165CB00001B/389